VIOLET OAKLANDER Ph.D.
2929 Glen Albyn Drive
Santa Barbara, CA 93105

D3

D1505178

THE GESTALT THERAPY BOOK

THE GESTALT THERAPY BOOK

A holistic guide to the theory, principles, and techniques of Gestalt therapy developed by Frederick S. Perls and others

JOEL LATNER, PH.D.

A PUBLICATION OF THE GESTALT JOURNAL

ISBN:
0-939266-03-2 clothbound
0-939266-04-0 softcover

Library of Congress Catalog Card Number: 85-070596

DEDICATED TO LAURIE, MY WIFE

We are the halves of a continent
That broke apart long ago
I have slowly crossed the oceans
As the currents push and the winds blow

Now we come together
I can feel our shorelines fitting in
Where I end
Is where you begin*

CONTENTS

Foreword

Gestalt therapy made its public debut in 1951 when Arthur Ceppos, owner of Julian Press, published *Gestalt Therapy: Excitement and Growth in the Human Personality* written by Frederick Perls, Ralph Hefferline and Paul Goodman. It would be more than two decades before another volume that elucidated the theory of Gestalt therapy would be published. Until 1973, when Joel Latner's *The Gestalt Therapy Book* and Erving and Miriam Polster's *Gestalt Therapy Integrated* appeared, little attention was paid to the theoretical foundations of Gestalt therapy.

During that twenty-two year period between 1951 and 1973, both the professional and general public heard and read much *about* Gestalt therapy, primarily due to the efforts of Frederick "Fritz" Perls to draw attention to it. Although a few serious articles appeared in professional journals and anthologies, Gestalt therapy became something to "do" rather than appreciate and understand. Through films that brought tears to the eye, audio tapes that revealed seemingly "instant" transformation and a book, *Gestalt Therapy Verbatim* (Perls, 1969), that consisted primarily of transcripts displaying a master clinician/theatrical director at work, Gestalt therapy became a media event.

According to a survey conducted by the American Academy of Psychotherapists in the early 1970's, Gestalt therapy was the most practiced of the "humanistic" psychotherapies. Everyone was "doing" it. Sadly enough, few knew what it was they were doing.

Happily, 1973 saw the beginning of a return to serious exploration of the principles of Gestalt therapy practice and *theory* with the appearance of the books by Latner and the Polsters. Frederick Perls had passed away, the spot light shown on other "stars" with different "cures." Gestalt therapy abandoned center stage and took its place among other "schools" of psychotherapy as one deserving careful study and serious consideration.

Fourteen more years have passed and during that time *The Gestalt Therapy Book* has become unavailable to the general public. Because we believe it to be an outstanding introduction to the principles of Gestalt therapy, an excellent initial choice for laymen, students and professionals, *The Gestalt Journal* decided to issue this revised edition.

Joe Wysong
Editor
The Gestalt Journal

Introduction to
The Gestalt Journal Edition

The history of this volume reflects the changes Gestalt therapy has undergone in public and professional awareness in the past fifteen years. *The Gestalt Therapy Book* was released in 1973 by the same small press which had published Perls, Hefferline and Goodman's landmark introduction of Gestalt therapy, *Gestalt Therapy: Excitement and Growth in the Human Personality* more than twenty years earlier. In the flush of those days, Gestalt therapy rode and rolled the crest of an intense and widespread interest in psychotherapy and personal growth on the basis of its novel and innovative methods, its radical perspective and its charismatic spokesman. In this atmosphere, *The Gestalt Therapy Book* was reprinted almost immediately as a mass market paperback and, like several other books on Gestalt therapy, distributed to nearly every bookstore in America and to book racks in supermarkets and major airports.

I was pleased but surprised at this. I had intended it as a readable introduction to the fundamentals of Gestalt therapy, a good place for professionals and the intelligent lay public to begin to understand the Gestalt approach. I had hoped it would become a cornerstone book in Gestalt therapy, but I never thought it would be a popular success — I thought the subject matter and my treatment of it too serious for that.

Most popular books have their fifteen minutes of stardom and fade into the ether, and *The Gestalt Therapy Book* was no exception. By the early eighties, it was no longer in print, a consequence of government regulations which discourage publishers from keeping slow selling titles in their warehouses, and more importantly I think, of the waning popularity of Gestalt therapy among the general public. Gestalt therapy is no longer a novelty, and psychological novelties are anyway not so popular as they once were.

If fashion has passed Gestalt therapy by, it is no less important for that. Its rich and perspicacious vantage point unite elements of life which are, in other psychologies, opposed or slighted. It is rooted in our biological nature, in our nervous systems, and at the same time recognizes that we are social creatures. It encompasses mind and body, psyche and the everyday worlds, feeling, thought, spirit, action, relationship. It gives the best accounting by far of our creative abilities, and in good hands is a remarkably effective way of helping us to live fully.

In this interim, with the spotlight elsewhere, some aspects of Gestalt therapy's theory and practice have been absorbed into the common fount of psychotherapeutic knowledge, a measure of its influence among professionals. Meanwhile, Gestalt therapists have settled down to the long haul of defining and refining our craft, teaching it to others, and doing what we can to awakened and enliven and enrich those who see us. It is in this new climate that *The Gestalt Therapy Book* has been given a new lease on life, a chance to provide an entree to Gestalt therapy for a new generation of readers to continue to make a contribution to these tasks.

I have largely resisted one opportunity which the prospect of a new edition affords: to revise the text to make it reflect what I have learned in the ensuing years. The exception is the two sections on the functions of the self, where my original discussion was so misconceived I had no choice. I think you will find the book entirely useful to you as it stands.

I feel more liberty, though, to revise the dedication. Now, eleven years further down our path, "Where I end/Is where you begin" is not nearly close enough. When the halves of a continent reunite, where any longer is the boundary between them?

Joel Latner

Rochester, New York
March, 1987

Acknowledgements

The basis of my understanding of Gestalt therapy is in my experience as a patient and my training at the Gestalt Institute of Cleveland. I want to thank my therapists, the teaching faculty at the institute, and my fellow trainees for their contributions to my education; especially Rainette Fantz, Erving and Miriam Polster, Joseph Zinker, Ed and Sonia Nevis, and William S. Warner. I also feel a debt to their teachers, to Fritz Perls, Laura Perls, Isadore From, Paul Weisz, and Paul Goodman. They developed Gestalt therapy and passed it on.

My patients and students have aided me immeasurably in the process of knowing and defining Gestalt therapy, which eventuated in this volume; and Elaine Kepner, John Weakland, Jim Green, and Erving Polster gave me valuable advice and assistance at an early stage in its genesis. Named and unnamed, I thank you all for your various contributions.

Finally, many other people in many places have made indirect but important contributions to this work through their participation in my welfare. In a way, no one and nothing can be excluded, but I think especially of friends and relations in New York City, Cleveland, Rochester, and the San Francisco Bay Area. They are the spokes and I am the wheel.

THE GESTALT THERAPY BOOK

Chapter 1
AN INTRODUCTION

The past few years have seen a great surge of public interest in psychology. Therapy groups are televised, a magazine devoted to psychology attracts more than a million subscribers, movies and books with psychological themes attract wide audiences. A significant and highly visible portion of the society turns to activities intended to promote personal development, interpersonal skills, spiritual growth, and self-understanding.

This new development is of a different order from the public consciousness about mental health and mental illness that has been growing steadily for many years. We have been examining emotional disturbances, child rearing, social problems, and education from a psychological viewpoint for several decades. Today we are seeing an increasing awareness that our own normal, well-adjusted lives could be richer than they are, and a growing interest in realizing that potential. The multitude of new schools of psychological theory and therapy, the encounter groups and growth games, the renewed interest in alternatives to traditional, problem-centered, and pathology-centered psychotherapy, the ready acceptance of esoteric spiritual systems are all part of this trend.

Developed in Europe, South Africa, and the United States in the thirties and forties, Gestalt therapy has been an influential component of this new force in psychology. On the West Coast, it is currently among the most utilized and emulated of the new psychologies. One of its founders was in residence at the Esalen Institute from its inception, and Gestalt therapy was until recently the "house" therapy at Esalen. The numerous Gestalt institutes here and in Canada are successful centers for professional training in Gestalt therapy and for personal growth activities.

The most visible aspect of Gestalt therapy is its techniques. Its forceful advocates have demonstrated their effectiveness in person and on film and tape before many thousands of lay and professional people. The Gestalt approach is called Gestalt *therapy*, underscoring its orientation to therapeutic change. Gestaltists are practical people, primarily concerned with helping people mature emotionally. They stress the hard work and rewards of personal growth, not speculation about it. This is of a piece with the centrality of activity, experience, and direct knowledge in Gestalt therapy and its awareness of the pitfalls of excessive intellection. Gestalt therapists tend to be activists, more interested in doing therapy than in talking about what they do.

As a result of this orientation to activity and the practical on the part of Gestalt practitioners, the literature of Gestalt therapy is small and strongly weighted toward applications of Gestalt principles to psychotherapy and other activities such as teaching and the arts. Relatively little of an explanatory or theoretical nature has been written. Gestalt therapists often organize their clinical material around theoretical or methodological principles; there are many digressions into various matters of theory contained in the published work on Gestalt therapy, and a few of them are concerned solely with theory. One of the two volumes of *Gestalt Therapy*, the basic book in Gestalt therapy, is devoted to theory, and it contains a wealth of provocative writing. But a clear and thorough explanation of the theoretical foundations of Gestalt therapy does not exist. This is the task I have addressed in *The Gestalt Therapy Book*.

If it is to be useful, a theory of human behavior ought to address these questions: What is mental health? What is mental illness?

What animates man, how does he function, and to what end? How does he get sick, and how does he get well? What is maturity, how does it occur, and how do we grow toward it? In what follows, I have presented the theory of Gestalt therapy in such a way that the interested reader can find out how these questions are answered from a Gestalt framework. The book also provides a context, a background, for understanding Gestalt writings and the many applications of Gestalt therapy. These are the principles that animate Gestaltists in their understanding of human behavior and their work. In the language of the hip seventies, this is where Gestalt therapy is coming from.

First Principles

Chinese lacquer box sets are constructed so that when we open the single box before us we find another box inside, instead of the empty space we expected. The box inside the one we opened is identical in shape and finish to the first box but it is slightly smaller; inside the second box is a third box; inside that one is a fourth, and so on.

In a way, each lacquer box follows from the one before it, since they fit together best when the proportions of any box are like the proportions of the one in which it rests. We can understand the relationship between the aspects of a theory of human behavior in the same way, since a theory works best when its parts follow in a consistent manner. We often say that a particular application of a general idea "comes out of" its general principles.

For example, it is basic to Gestalt therapy that we are healthy when we are in touch with ourselves, our environment and the relationship between them. Based on that principle, we can conceive of illness or abnormality: we are unhealthy when we are out of touch with ourselves and our environment. And a further step in this progression — opening another box — is the conception of treatment implied in these preceding statements: regaining our health is a matter of restoring the awareness we have lost. Next are particular procedures or techniques for increasing awareness. These concepts are joined together by a continuing focus on the importance of awareness, and the logical and practical connections between theory and practice, diagnosis and treatment.

In the example of our Chinese boxes, we can see that the dimensions of every box in the set are determined by the dimensions of the first, largest box, because they fit together best when they are identical in proportion to it. (It is possible to consider the smallest box as the first in the sequence; however, the point remains the same.) Going back to our Gestalt example, we can place the statements about awareness within each other in the same way. "Particular techniques" goes into "treatment," which goes into "illness," which goes into "health"; this last-named box goes inside one labeled "the Gestalt theory of human behavior." We find we have two boxes left, and the one marked "Gestalt theory" will fit into the remaining box, which is marked "first principles."

First principles are statements of what is important and what is unimportant in how we perceive and organize things. They are principles of construction and selection. In the case of our boxes, it is important that they fit inside one another as closely as possible. (It is not important, for example, that they are watertight.) The first principles of a theory are the guidelines that determine what must be included and accounted for in the theory and what can be ignored and left out. Simply, first principles are statements of the theory-maker's interests. More formally, first principles are epistemological rules.

Epistemology is concerned with knowledge and the different kinds of rules that are made to decide when we know something. For example, physicists have decided that, for them, knowledge consists of information about the atomic structure of matter; for sociologists, knowledge is information about man's social relations; for Marxists, it is information about the relationships between economic, political, and social conditions. In a way, epistemology is about the different cross sections people take of reality.

First Principles of Gestalt Therapy

The foundation of the first principles of Gestalt therapy is holism. The essence of the holistic conception of reality is that all nature is a unified and coherent whole. The organic and inorganic elements of the universe exist together in a continually changing process of coordinating activity. Each of these elements, in any scale — a plant, a continent, a child, a sunflower, an alga — is itself a coordinated integral process imbedded in the larger whole. We ourselves are an intimate part of this palpitating universe. At the same time that they appear to be discrete, objects and events participate in the unity formed of their relationships to other objects and events.

A holistic understanding of man, for example, brings the functioning of his physical body, his emotions, his thoughts, his culture, and his social expressions into a unified picture. They are all aspects of the same event — man. The mind does not cause the body to operate, nor the body the mind; to conceive of things in that way is to emphasize their separateness. Instead, the pounding of our heart, our excitement, and the concurrent anxiety are manifestations of the same occurrence, like heat and light from the sun. Holistically, we cannot understand ourselves by summing our understanding of our heart, our brain, our nervous system, our limbs, our circulatory system. We are not simply an accumulation of functions. The ordinary language expression for this is: The whole is greater than the sum of its parts. "Greater" means different in quality from; it also refers to the entirety of the object or event. Therefore, the whole is a new event, as water is greater than two parts of hydrogen and one part of oxygen, and a hand is greater than four fingers and a thumb.

The principal characteristics of Gestalt epistemology and theory come from holism. For instance, we are more interested in integration than analysis. Because we are looking for the ways in which things come together, we attempt to understand them in ways that bring them together, rather than in ways that separate them. Therefore, we are attuned more to the processes and principles that reoccur in behavior than to the temporary forms these processes take. We are more interested in the dynamics of behavior, the music of living, than we are in static forms. Take this example, this series of dots:

```
      .   .
    .       .
    .   .   .
    .
    .
```

Though there are actually some dots on the page, we see a P. This occurs because the following principle or organization is built into our perceptual apparatus: We order the world as we contact it, making sense of the reality in the process of sensing it. As holists, we are interested in this process of making a whole — a P

— out of the dots on the page. That is the music. We are less interested in the particular fixed form, the P, that issues from this process. Another illustration: Holistically, we are more interested in the artist's activity as he creates than we are in any particular piece of art he creates.

The visual example cited above is also an instance of the way that holistic functioning is more than a convenient abstraction — it also corresponds to important aspects of reality, and holism draws veracity and support from the accuracy of the fit it makes with the world we experience. The importance of our ability to see dots as the letter P is that it is intrinsic to our behavior as human beings that we organize the bits around us into wholes. We must do it; it is part of our nature. The holistic occupation with the principles of organization that underlie the process of our living — trying to find the aspects of man that determine what he — trying to find the aspects of man that determine what he is capable of — is called structuralism. By "structure" we mean some quality of our functioning that is reflected in regularities of behavior and in definite characteristics of our physical selves. If we can know them, we know something of man's nature. A part of our visual system, for example, consists of cones in the retina of the eye that are sensitive only to movements in the visual field. They insure that we are attentive to what is new and changing. This structural principle can be found in the rest of our sensory and motor systems and in our emotional and intellectual processes, and we can conclude that it is characteristic of us as organisms that we are attuned to novelty. (We can think of these structures as man's built-in epistomology, for they comprise his rules for knowing the world.)

If we think holistically, we know that any whole we examine is tied to the rest of the multivariate universe. As a consequence, when we study processes, we must study their contexts, or we shall leave something out. Take this example:

$$
\begin{array}{cccc}
3 & 2 & & \\
2 & 1 & & \\
\rule{1cm}{0.4pt} \quad 1 & 0 & V & E \\
2 & 1 & & \\
3 & 2 & &
\end{array}
$$

Is the first figure in the indicated line a one, or an el? Is the second a zero, or an oh? The answer, of course, is that it depends. In the context of LOVE, they are letters. In the context of

2 1

1 0

2 1

they are numbers.

Since part of the context of any event or object we know about is the one who is knowing, we understand the seeker after knowledge in a special way from a holistic perspective. There is no "objective" knowledge and no "subjective" knowledge, for there are no objects and no subjects; the terms imply that the object is separate from the subject and knows it, objectively. Holistically, though, the observer is part of the context of the subject, since we must make contact with what we want to know about in order to know it. There are no outside events, and no impersonal subjects. A holistic approach includes our awareness of what we know.

> Biologists have shown that the organism constantly inter-acts with its environment. The view that it submits passively to the environment has become untenable. How then can man be simply a recorder of outside events? When he transforms his environment by acting on it he gains a deeper knowledge of the world than any copy of reality could ever provide.
>
> *Piaget*

We cannot be detached men of science, watching what happens from a distance. We must be aware of ourselves and in-volved in what we are attempting to know. Investigation is not dis-passionate; but as Laing pointed out, this is essential if a science of human behavior is to be adequate to its subject. We need our ex-perience to make meaning of what we encounter, and we cannot know another's humanity if we cannot touch it with our own.

The results of holistic inquiry and theory-making have dis-tinctive qualities. One of them is an emphasis on knowing things by describing what we encounter. The principle of explanation we use is detailed description of the object or event, including its context. We want to know *how* things happen, in what context, with what effect. This is a present-centered activity. If we asked *why* instead of *how*, we would look to the past for causes, but the holistic approach, stressing the activity itself and its context, eschews history in favor of the here-and-now. The emphasis is on phenomena, on the present as it can be known through empathy, observation, and experience. Things are explained by their existence as we know them, by description. Descriptions are a way of answering relevant questions.

Gestalt therapy is a theory of behavior based on the holistic epistomology I have outlined. It is descriptive, integrative, and structural, emphasizing phenomenology and the present. It is these things because its theory of knowledge is also these things. The therapy that follows from the theory shares them as well. It is a consistent approach to the phenomenal world — knowledge, theory, and practice.

A Caveat and a Suggestion

This is the basis of the theory of behavior that is called Gestalt therapy. The way it provides of approaching the world is the hallmark of the Gestalt approach to human behavior, psychotherapy, and living. Though some of its proponents say it is the way we know naturally, it is also important to remember that we are talking about a theory of knowledge and a theory of behavior. We are talking about theories, not the real world. Not "it." If we keep this in mind, we will not, in Bassui's terms, mistake the menu for the dinner.

If the theory laid out in these pages is apt, it suggests away of dealing with occurrences that seems true, for now, and that works for us. If it is well done, it has the truth of art, a finger on the pulse. But a theory is ". . . a working hypothesis, an auxiliary construct that we build and adhere to for the purpose of communication, rationalization, and justification of our particular personal approach" (L. Perls, undated, p. 2).

Theories are approximations, both more and less precise than what they refer to. By their nature, they stumble on the abnormalities of experience, the exceptions and individual cases that highlight the uniqueness of existence. Looking for patterns and clarity, the theories we build bear the same relation to what they refer to as Cezanne's cubes do to the provincial farmhouses that were his subjects. A good theory is an illuminating metaphor, with a life of its own and a relation to its subject that augments both. But we should remind ourselves that any theory also fixes the flow of life with immutable words, representing reality with mental constructions and their relationships. It is like putting shoes on a snake.

The chapter that follows this introduction contains basic information about the Gestalt approach. Its origins in natural processes is described in some detail, for all the concepts out of which the theory of Gestalt therapy is constructed come from them. These fundamental principles are developed in the next chapter, on the Gestalt understanding of healthy human behavior. Chapter 4 describes how our functioning is disrupted and destroyed and Chapter 5 describes the Gestalt methodology for restoring healthy behavior. Limitations, changes, and new possibilities are discussed in the last chapter, and an annotated bibliography of Gestalt writings concludes this volume.

The format and style of the "Book" is that of a tour or a presentation, ushering the reader through the intricacies and attractions of Gestalt therapy. There are many things here. Some of them will interest you, others will not. Here it is, take a look.

Chapter 2
BASIC PRINCIPLES

We believe the Gestalt outlook is the original, undistorted, natural approach to life; that is, to man's thinking, feeling, acting.

PERLS, HEFFERLINE, GOODMAN

Gestalt therapy starts with nature. Its inspiration and its basic principles are taken from looking at free functioning in nature, in our body, and in our healthy spontaneous behavior. The dynamics of nature and of man are of a piece, and we can use what we observe to construct a theory of human behavior. Gestalt therapy is organized around principles of biological structure and functioning that can be seen in natural behavior. "Gestalt is as ancient and old as the world itself" (F. S. Perls, 1969b, p. 16), because it is based on the principles of organization that animate life.

Organismic Self-Regulation

Organisms — people, animals, plants — have specific needs that must be met if they are to live. Our bodies require a certain amount of moisture for optimal functioning, and we die if the deficiency or excess is too great. In the course of our activities, we use up some of the water we have taken in through sweating and evaporation, and through urination. The amount of water in us falls below the level we need for good functioning. We get thirsty, and we find a way to restore the level of water in our systems to its optimum level. At the same time, we are likely to deplete the amount of salt present in our bodies, and we will find a way to take in salt to restore the balance of our metabolic system — perhaps seeking out salty foods, or salting what we eat more heavily than usual. This is true for all the elements of nature that we need to live and grow: proteins, minerals and vitamins, sensory stimulation, movement, affection, sleep. And it is true for all living things: When deficiencies exist, the organic system remedies them; when excesses are present, it rids itself of them.

In Gestalt therapy, this general principle is called organismic self-regulation. "The organism is striving for the maintenance of an equilibrium which is continuously disturbed by its needs and regained through their gratification or elimination" (F. S. Perls, 1947, p. 7).

This integrated and coherent mode of operating in the world can be observed in all living things, and all the subsystems that make up organisms. Our cells contribute to our unified functioning, and they are also in and of themselves unified and organized self-regulating wholes. Organismic self-regulation is how Gestalt therapy refers to this complex process of attaining, losing, and regaining biological balance.

The principle of organismic self-regulation is not an instinct theory, but it is related to that earlier, simpler idea. The difference is one of sophistication and emphasis. Instinct theories claim we drink because we have an instinct for water. This is mechanistic explanation, creating things — instincts — within us that make us behave in a certain way and creating a division between us and our "instincts." Organismic self-regulation is a holistic representation of a complex biological process, a description of the orchestration of many needs of the organism in its behavior. We drink when we need water. Creating a water instinct is a response to the need to explain why we drink; so, we make up a mechanism to make us want to drink. But self-regulation is not a mechanism, it is a process.

Another way of stating this principle of organismic self-regulation is that the organism functions with a prudence born of its needs and their fulfillment. Unless their ability to regulate themselves is disturbed — which happens regularly with humans and domesticated animals, and rarely elsewhere — organisms show a wisdom and economy in their behavior. Animals eat only what they need and no more. Left to their own lights, they do not run amuck, but are careful and judicious. Writings in ethology, the study of animals in their natural environs, are full of instances of the restraint, social organization, and cooperation that come out of organismic self-regulation; gratuitous killing, for example, is completely absent in "wild" animals. Organismic self-regulation is the wisdom of these interactions. On the human level, organismic self-regulation is Rank's belief that the self has within its essential nature the capacity to cope, to be in harmony with itself. This is in contrast to the psychoanalytic notion that structurally man is in conflict with himself, and health is the domination of the self by the most worthy part.

Implicit in organismic self-regulation is the idea that organisms have awareness. In order to know their own balance and to find and obtain what they need to meet imbalances, organisms must be aware of themselves. Fulfilling needs occurs when the need is present; it is not automatic. The organism is an open, self-resetting system in touch with itself. Automatic behavior, like eating three balanced meals a day at eight, twelve, and six, does not require awareness. It is a closed system, programmed in advance. But seeking out the means to gratify needs as they arise requires awareness.

Awareness is used here in the sense of apprised of, knowing, having information about. It does not necessarily imply consciousness. We are aware of the force of gravity and its relation to our movements as we walk, without knowing that we know that, or being able to articulate it. Every child knows that, before it is able to speak or conceptualize. Frederick S. Perls, one of the founders of Gestalt therapy, believed that awareness in this sense was an aspect of all existence, organic and inorganic, along with time and space. "I am sure that one day we will discover that awareness is a property of the universe — extension, duration, awareness" (1970b, p. 29). He believed that all nature is bound together by a mutual sensitivity and responsiveness. This ought not to seem farfetched, even in the case of inorganic matter. Many of us can acknowledge the effect that events have on our physical surroundings, the "vibes" that a room or a place absorb from what has gone on in it. Research has been done on the reactions of plants and rocks to emotional events. In both cases, measurable changes in their magnetic fields have been recorded in the presence of articulations of various emotions — the fields of rocks change when they are cursed out. (There is a short story by Roald Dahl about a writer who dropped a live microphone accidentally on grass being cut and was astonished to hear the grass screaming.)

The principle of organismic self-regulation does not imply or ensure the satisfaction of the needs of the organism. It implies that organisms will do their best to regulate themselves, given their own capabilities and the resources of the environment. The principle is similar to the Gestalt psychology principle of *pregnanz*: "Any psychological field is as well organized as the global conditions will permit at that particular time." For example, in the course of his maturation, a tall boy may learn to stoop his back and shoulders to avoid humiliation and embarrassment. His perception is that his environment will not support him if he stands up to his full height. His posture, of course, is poor, but given what he feels are the circumstances, it is the best that can be managed. Organismic self-regulation does not ensure health, only that the organism does all it can with what is available.

The Relationship of the Organism and the Environment

In the context of organismic self-regulation, the relationship between the organism and its environment is a critical one. The organism and the environment comprise an interdependent unity in which the organism is striving to regulate itself. "Every organism needs an environment to exchange essential substances — air, love" (F. S. Perls, 1969a,p.5).

Saying that the organism needs the environment is not precise or complete enough. The organism is imbedded in the environment, as much a part of it as a spoke is of a wheel. Understanding the existence and function of the organism is predicated upon understanding its relationship to and functioning in the field. The relationship is analogous to the ties between family members. The existence of one member is bound up with the existence of the others; the ties cannot be broken, or disallowed, or chosen. We can choose to some extent the kind of environment we wish, but we cannot choose not to relate at all. Even after we die, we continue to relate to the environment until we become indivisible from it.

The life of the organism depends on its relations with its environment. Every few seconds we disturb the oxygen balance in our systems through metabolic action and are required to return to the environment and make an exchange with it, giving off the carbon dioxide we cannot use and taking in the fresh air we require. Similarly, we need the field to satisfy our needs to love, to create and destroy things, to take our anger and our affection and our concern, to test our skills and our courage. "Most emotions require the world as object, or do not satisfy" (F.S. Perls,1947,p.117).

Organisms have two systems that assist in their interactions with the environment. The sensory or orientation system is the organization of faculties that receive information about the environment. Our eyes, our ears, our skin and nose are part of our orientation systems. So are the receptors in our bodies. The motor system is the organization of manipulative faculties. It permits the organism to make changes in its environment, or changes in its relationship to it.

At first glance, it might appear that the orienting system is passive and receptive, taking in the world, and the manipulating system is active and aggressive. It might also appear that the organism is first stimulated in its orienting system by the environment and then responds motorically to that stimulation. The actual situation is that both systems, the system of orientation and the system of manipulation, can reach out to the environment from the organism. This situation obtains because the organism is not indiscriminate in its sensory relation to the environment. Rather, its perceptions are structured: It sees certain aspects of the environment and not others. It reaches out to grasp the things it needs.

I look up from my writings, noticing I am thirsty, and I think about getting a drink of water; going into the kitchen, I pour a full glass of water, drain it, and return to my desk. I notice it is sunny and cool in the room where I am writing; the cats are playing with each other and there is traffic passing by outside. All of these were as true a few minutes ago as they are now, but I did not notice them then. I ignored them, reaching out to the deficit of moisture in my body and then to the water faucet, and my manipulative system organized around the water. There are many possibilities in my environment, but I organized around my thirst, in preference to the other possibilities. I was not stimulated randomly and passively by the field; rather my senses organized around my thirst.

While our sensory and motor systems can reach out to the environment, the reverse is also true. The environment can reach out, demanding that we be attentive to what is occurring there; and we will be attentive, providing that we are capable of it. The organism and the environment contact each other and interact in a process of mutual accommodation that in Gestalt therapy is called creative adjustment. Organismic self-regulation is the organism's process of making creative adjustments within its field.

Organismic self-regulation implies that the organism will be able to gratify its needs provided that resources of the environment permit it. Healthy functioning — the realization of the full potential of the organism — requires environmental support. Without it, the organism cannot maintain itself. If environmental support is meager, the organism will not have all its needs met, and the absence of environmental support is a fatal crisis for it. Seen another way, if the field cannot maintain itself with the organism as part of it, the organism will be destroyed by the field.

The Middle Mode

At times in our lives, many of us have had the experience of giving ourselves over to some ongoing experience. Perhaps losing track of time in the midst of creative activity, or permitting the flood of our excitement to carry us, with some surprise, into a new experience of orgasm, even in a simple meeting with a friend, our words pour out of us with a facility that pleases and astonishes us.

In describing this kind of experience, the language we can command is often awkward and imprecise, especially when we try to ascribe responsibility. To say "I wrote this poem" is, in one sense, perfectly correct. After all, no one else wrote it; and poems do not just happen — someone must write them. But it often seems more apt to say, "it just happened," not because we didn't "do" it, but because it seems both inaccurate and even a little prideful to be responsible for this spontaneous event in the same way that we do the dishes or start the car.

Current popular expressions, like "Let it happen," are in touch with this aspect of our experience, the experience of spontaneous behavior. Here is Fellini:

> I prepare everything . . . but then I want the film to grow and tell me what I must do. This is not improvising; this is humble service to a creature of one's own that is growing and has its own needs.

We are completely present in the experience, we are involved, acting, but we are aware that the felicity and excitement of the event owes those qualities to something other than our intentions, or our wills, or the intentions of other participants. After all, in good lovemaking, it simply isn't the case that the mutuality, pleasure, and climatic excitement come from our plans about it. (Often they occur in spite of them.) We are not doing; nor are we being done to. We are neither active, nor passive — both, really, and yet not either. It is the wisdom of the Tao: Stand out of the way.

Our difficulty in expressing the nature of this kind of human experience owes itself to what Goodman calls "a disease of language" (Perls, Hefferline, and Goodman, 1951, p. 376). In the structure of English, we are obliged to divide what we wish to talk about into subjects and objects. Subjects do things to objects, or objects do things to subjects. "I take your hand" or "I am insulted by you." In the active and passive voices in English, things that are separate from each other take action upon other things.

The alternative is the intransitive voice. "It happened," or "It is raining." "It fell." Here we convey that an event occurred with no attribution of involvement or responsibility at all. So in speaking of the things that comprise living in this universe, the interior and exterior events and the relationships between them, we must speak in these ways — actively, passively, or intransitively. You move me, or, I am moved by you, or, it somehow happened that we were moved. We resort to awkward devices or graceful metaphors (depending on our skills) in trying to be precise and expressive about acts that seem to be our doing and yet experientially not completely our doing.

The difficulty comes from a bias in our language. Phenomena must be described in a language that separates events into subjects and objects, connecting them only in the active, passive, or intransitive modes. What we create and what exists must be related so that subjects and objects do things to each other linearly, one after the other; or else they must not be related at all — things just happen. We can talk of what we will and intend, and the results of our willful acts, and of things that happen without our participation. The bias is that our language tools are better for talking about interactions between separate entities than between related ones. They seem to cast all events into a mold that emphasizes the separation of things rather than their integration.

This bias is deeply imbedded in the thinking and world view of our culture. We see it in many places; in the kind of science we have, in politics and social affairs. Political intercourse, for example, has come to be the meeting of separate wills negotiating compromises so as to allow the parties to live together. Subject acts on object, thing on thing. There is no caring and no compassion, just objects colliding. And as these political conflicts are the analogs of the passive and active voices, the apathy, acquiescence, helplessness, and alienation of the uninvolved live out the intransitive mode. Other possibilities are hard to think of — and how would we speak of them?

In other languages — Greek, for example — there is a voice that is called the middle mode. The middle mode permits us to speak of spontaneous and integrated activity appropriately, in a way that entails the integration and wholeness that is the central aspect of that behavior. "The middle mode . . . refers the process to itself as a totality; it feels it as its own and is engaged in it" (Perls, Hefferline, and Goodman, 1951, p.376).

The middle mode enables us to add another nuance to speaking and thinking of behavior and relationships. We can talk directly and accurately of them, implying the holistic mutual interpenetration of all the aspects of experience. The middle mode is the voice of unified events. It is the modality of expression that best represents the present-centered, phenomenological orientation to knowledge and events on which Gestalt therapy depends.

The middle mode is also the appropriate way to speak of emotional functioning. Feelings are not willed by us, nor can we be compelled to feel something. At the same time, they are ours; they do not rain down on us. Feelings issue forth from us. We are involved in them, they *are* us at the time. They are middle mode events.

In the discussion of aspects of organismic free functioning that constitutes this chapter, and throughout this Book, these processes we are talking about are middle mode processes. The language we use to talk about them is not — it cannot be — but it is the middle mode of experience and behavior that is implied throughout.

Gestalt Formation: Figure and Background

Organismic self-regulation is a continuing process of distinguishing the needs of the organism and the means whereby those needs can be gratified, organizing them into a cohesive whole of comprehension and activity, and carrying out that activity to its satisfying conclusion. At that time, the unified organismic functioning that came about as a result of the organismic imbalance will disappear. The organism rebalances itself. This process repeats again and again for the duration of any organism's existence — indeed, this process *is* the living of the organism.

In Gestalt therapy, the undifferentiated field — the unity of organism and environment — is called the background, or ground. The emerging focus of attention and activity is called the figure, or gestalt*, and what does not become part of that focus remains background. The process of forming foci of attention and activity is called gestalt formation, or figure formation; the process of gratification and disappearance of needs and their attendant gestalts is called gestalt destruction or figure destruction.

There is no exact equivalent in English for the German word *gestalt*. A gestalt is a whole, a pattern, a configuration, a cohesive one, a form that cannot be broken down without destroying it. It is the pattern of the gestalt that is indivisible; the relationship between the parts cannot change without destroying the particular gestalt. Even though the parts themselves may change, if the relationships are the same, the gestalt will remain intact. A marriage is a whole. Two people, any two, who relate to each other in a certain way, are married. They are part of a marriage. "The whole determines the parts. It is not merely the sum total" (Perls, Hefferline, and Goodman, 1951, p. xi).

---

*The word is from the German. It is pronounced variously. The *g* is hard. The first syllable rhymes with "yes"; the *s*, however, is pronounced as *sh*. In German, the last syllable requires an *a* sound that does not exist in English between the *a* in altitude and the *a* in hall (or the *au* in fault) — a little shorter than the *a* in psalm. Most Gestaltists Americanize it, so the " — talt" rhymes with salt.

Or take this illustration:

```
        X                        O
  X  X  X  X  X           O  O  O  O  O
        X                        O
        X                        O
        X                        O
        X                        O
```

Here the gestalt is a cross. Whether composed of the letter x or the letter o, the gestalt remains a cross.
Similarly in the case of a melody:

Here the keys are different. Only one note in the first melody fragment is also in the second fragment. They have only a G-natural in common, and yet the gestalt is the same, they are the same melody.

In Gestalt therapy, as in Gestalt psychology*, gestalt formation is considered a primary characteristic of organismic function-

---

*Gestalt psychology was a major influence on Fritz and Laura Perls in their formulation of Gestalt therapy. Laura Perls was a student of Wertheimer, who was a leading figure in Gestalt psychology. In an interview, Fritz Perls stated he had read only a few papers by the Gestalt psychologists, taking a few ideas from them. The ones he took, however, are among the pivotal aspects of Gestalt therapy: closure, and gestalt figure/ground formation.

ing. It is in the nature of organisms, a part of their being, that they form gestalts. Forming gestalts is primary in perception and in understanding; they precede any analysis of the constituent parts of the gestalt. In the beginning we see in wholes, and then we differentiate.

There are qualities that, by observation and experiment, have been found to characterize gestalts. In classical Gestalt psychology, these qualities of form included the aforementioned *pregnanz*, closure, good continuation or good form, proximity and similarity. Take closure, for example. We require that gestalts have the quality of being whole, or finished. Given this series of dots,

.

.   .

we see a triangle. We need to organize the field so that it makes sense to us and still respects the given field — and making sense means making gestalts. Another example is the familiar story of the salesman who went to sleep in a hotel. Shortly after he retired, he was awakened by the footsteps of his noisy neighbor. Then he heard the muffled thud of a shoe hitting the floor of his neighbor's bedroom — then, silence. After twenty-five minutes of increasing frustration and irritation, the salesman got up, went to the next room, and pounded on the door, awakening his neighbor to ask him testily what happened to the other shoe.

There are other common grounds of Gestalt therapy and Gestalt psychology. They share the same holistic structuralist perspective of man, and though Gestalt therapy is indebted to many other approaches as well, a grasp of Gestalt psychology is perhaps the simplest and most direct way to understand the underpinnings of Gestalt therapy. The Gestalt psychologists concentrated on man's perception; Gestalt therapy extends the Gestalt psychologists' discoveries about external perception to encompass all human perception, and uses the same principles to understand the full range of human behavior.

In Gestalt therapy, concerned with total organismic behavior and not only perception, gestalts are strong or weak, graceful or forced, clear or diffused, lively or dull. If orgasmic functioning is unimpaired, gestalts are lively and strong and clear and graceful.

Gestalt formation is the creation of a figure in a field. The field is always present. Though the field may recede in importance (and even seem to disappear altogether momentarily) as the gestalt comes to the center of our attention, gestalt formation occurs in the context of the field, like the melody of a raga differentiates itself from the drone that supports it, and to which it returns. The figure/ground relationship is a differentiation of part of the field into a place of centrality and importance, without losing touch with the rest of the field. This is holistic differentiation — the gestalt is a manifestation of the field, sharp and clear and distinct, and yet imbedded in its background. "The greatest cutting does not sever," says the Tao Te Ching.

A gestalt is what is concernful and interesting to us. It is what our organismic self-regulation requires. Stated another way, what is meaningful to us becomes a gestalt. These terms refer to different aspects of the same process. Gestalt formation is the creation of figures that the organism values in the process of gratifying its needs. Gestalt formation is the organism creating meaning out of the field. The basis of values is in gestalt formation. Meaning is created *ad hoc*, because of a context and a need. When I was thirsty, relieving my thirst had meaning and value; now, in the context of my interests and ambitions, this writing has meaning and value.

The gamut of emotional experience is also based in figure/ground formation and destruction. As we interact in the field, attempting to follow through our best interests, our different aspects respond in their characteristic ways, as part of our total organismic activity: our cognitive faculties think, our senses feel, our motor system acts, our affective level of being responds with qualities we experience as emotions. These are different man-ifestations of our organization in the field. If we become afraid, our fear *is* our fevered attempts to figure out what to do, our rapid breathing, our contact with what frightens us, and our actions. They are all part of the totality of that event, issuing forth as part of the dynamics of the figure/ground phenomenon.

The judgment that we make in any circumstance about what is most important and what we shall respond to is the wisdom of the organism about its own needs. So also are the selections we make from the environment as we attempt to meet them. The first judgment that the organism makes is a process called spontaneous dominance. What is spontaneously dominant in free functioning is the top of the need hierarchy of urgency at that time. It is what the organism judges it must attend to, now. The ethics and motivation of the organism arise out of the spontaneous dominance. The organism is following its needs, marshaling the energy that it has at its disposal for dealing with what is most important to it. Only what is spontaneously dominant can marshal the single-mindedness that is a necessary aspect of good figure formation. Following any other interest — perhaps because the organism is forced to — means the organism must restrain its natural impulse to attend to what dominates its attention, and the energy of that restraint is lost to its engagement with the emerging gestalt.

This judgment is not the judgment of a court, carefully weighing the issues of law and circumstance; nor is it compulsion or willfulness or persuasion. It is the judgment of air filling a vacuum, of sleeping when we are tired. It has the quality of inevitability — a total organismic act of preference as opposed to the solely cognitive one of making decisions. Spontaneous dominance flows with artistic fatality out of the organism and its environment.

Predifferentiation or Indifference, and Divided Attention

Thinking about our behavior, we can see that the description laid out above doesn't fit all cases. We are capable of attending to more than one thing at a time. We can also force ourselves to attend to what does not interest us, excluding things we would prefer to attend to.

In discussing this, it is useful to distinguish between a split gestalt and the state of predifferentiated awareness. In the latter, we are not aware of anything in particular, but we are open to the field in general. There is no present center of attention, no business at hand. We are cruising. In this state, we are balanced, existing at a zero point of gratification where we lack nothing and have no surplus. Perhaps we have had this experience on a vacation, after the satisfaction of a good meal or lovemaking subsides, or when the afterglow of finishing something we have worked on wholeheartedly is diminishing. Also called the state of creative indifference, it is part of the process of gestalt formation and destruction, the point after a figure has been destroyed and before one begins to form.

We are also capable of listening to the radio while driving, eating, and reading, shaving, and planning our day. This is a different state from the one I just described. In this state, our attention is divided, our energies are split. We have a conflict in what is dominant; instead of resolving the conflict, we do both. The two (or more) figures go on simultaneously, each of them claiming part of ourselves. In this state, we necessarily create weak, diffuse gestalts. Lacking the immediacy, power, and satisfaction of unified gestalts, these experiences do not command the involvement that a strong figure does. Some of this splitting is inevitable, but it is no less taxing and unsatisfying for that. It is akin to neurotic conflict, where we constantly fight a limited war with ourselves; although these activities can go on side by side and not render us immobile, our experience has the same vapidness that characterizes so much of neurotic experience.

Similar to this is the situation where we feel a conflict of interests that we resolve by choosing one or the other. Perhaps our indecision comes because both seem to be equally desirable, or equally undesirable, and the conflict seems torturous. From the point of view of gestalt formation this situation obtains when we are not yet aware of all the aspects of the coming gestalt. Deciding at this point, "making" a choice, short-circuits the natural process of finding our preference. It imposes an artificial outcome that stands apart from the wisdom of the organism and its total functioning. As in the case of split gestalts, this is to be distinguished from the emergence of spontaneous dominance that comes from nature left to its own devices.

Conceptions of Nature and the Natural

In Gestalt therapy, human nature is considered to be flexible. In part, it is given, and in part it is constantly created according to circumstances. It is both given in the structures of our being and formed by our interaction with the environment and in the mutuality of creative adjustments.

What is given in human nature are those aspects that define us as human beings. Reich writes, "What is called 'nature in man', then, can be taken out of the realm of the mystics and poetic fantasy and can be translated into the concrete language of natural science. It is not a matter of metaphysics or analogies, nor of sentimental perception, but of concrete, visible and manageable processes of the living"(1960c, p. 186). What is given are the structures that organize our living: organismic self-regulation, gestalt formation, and the figure/ground relationship, spontaneous dominance — the processes of free functioning described above.

These are givens. At the same time, they are potentialities open to manifold uses. Human nature is created again and again by each of us as we realize ourselves today and as we have realized ourselves in the past. Even the natural structures can be modified, subsumed, and subverted in the course of our living. We can create second natures that come to seem natural to us, although they contravene the structural givens that are our own best interests. Human nature cannot be so easily sorted out from behavior. At the same time, the structures that I have described define our possibilities. We must relate to them even in contradicting them, because they are always present. We have a grain. We can go against it, but it exists and makes the going rough.

This conception of man's nature is Aristotelian. Man is not naturally good or bad, as Rousseau on the one hand or Hobbes on the other believed. Man has a way of being which best suits his make-up — it *is* his make-up. In Gestalt therapy, it is called free functioning. It is a premise of Gestalt therapy that it is good for men to be what is intrinsic to them. To be human is to live according to these structures, for they are our human qualities. The problem and challenge of our life is to find a way to fulfill our humanity.

In a way, questions of goodness and morality are superfluous. The issue is whether we shall realize our possibilities or deny them. At the same time, any serious consideration of man must acknowledge that going against our grain is epidemic, and an understanding of our natures must acknowledge that as being part of our natures too. That potentiality must even be anticipated if a statement about human nature is to be adequate to the facts.

Destruction and Aggression

Created out of organismic need in the context of the field, gestalts persist as long as they fulfill or attempt to fill an organismic need. When they cease to have any reason for being, they are destroyed and forgotten. When a gestalt is said to be destroyed, the phrase means it can no longer be found in the form that defined it as that particular gestalt. Its components may exist — they must exist in some form since matter cannot be destroyed — but the particular figure that was formed at a particular time as part of organismic self-regulation disappears. I was thirsty, and I obtained and drank the water I needed. The figure of satisfying by thirst dissolves as the water disappears within me and begins to be transformed into my body tissues.

Both gestalt formation and destruction are the working out of structural processes intrinsic to existence. In the process of living, we must create and destroy. These processes are aggressive ones. They do not happen by themselves. They require our active participation. The formation of a gestalt is an act of creation, its disappearance is an act of destruction; both are aggressive acts.

Destruction, then, is basic to living and natural functioning. The Lowara gypsies say, "Without wood, the fire would die." If we are to eat, we must destroy the food we have, changing its form from food to our body tissues by a process of cutting, tearing, grinding, dissolving. To destroy something is to trans-form it, to change the gestalt to another. Plants, insects, and animals destroy each other in the course of their own living. Life is a cycle of creation and destruction, a succession of deaths and births. To support ourselves, we must eat. Far from the supermarket — where food seems to spring forth already packaged from inert and neutral materials — plants and animals are killed so they can be destroyed by us, so we can live. When we die, we eventually become food for insects and plants, and they the food for the animal and plant that will sustain our children's children. In Gestalt therapy the aggressiveness that is entailed in differentiating the field into figure and ground and that eventuates in the destruction of the gestalt is recognized and valued as an essential aspect of organismic self-regulation.

In our culture, where violence is entertainment and murder is public policy, it is difficult to value aggression and destruction. The conventional wisdom urges us to get along with one another, and to eschew conflict and rancor. We learn to be compliant. Aggression and destruction become loaded words, auguring the dissolution of our controls, threatening chaos and the possibility of losing ourselves in the flood of our anger. This is not the free functioning of aggression and destruction. It is a collective insanity stemming in part from an estrangement from those natural processes in their unhindered form. As we shall see later on, the basic processes described in this section can come to our ruin. Left to themselves, they permit us to realize ourselves; disrupted and repressed, they persist, taking the familiar forms of behavior we see around us and the tragedies of the daily newspapers and of history. But the free interplay of the organism and the environment and the process of creating and destroying figures, "comes not to chaos or mad fantasy, but to a gestalt that solves a real problem."

The Gestalt Conception of Reality

In Gestalt therapy, reality is understood to have the same quality to it that is in nature, the physical universe, and in interactions: partly it is given, and partly it is malleable.

We have seen previously that our worlds are made of what is important to us. What is figure for us is what we know or want. The rest, phenomenologically, does not exist. We create the world for ourselves according to our needs, organizing it as we live out the interplay of figure and ground. When we are interested, we are aware of what is present, as it is part of the process of discovery and invention that is the creative adjustment of the organism and the environment. Reality in this sense is flexible and changing. We make it anew continually as we live.

At the same time, we also know that the events and objects we leave behind when we are done with them maintain an independent existence. They reoccur, and we in our phenomenology incorporate the reoccurrence into our understanding of the world. There is a world that goes on without us — what is called an objective world. We can even say that the worlds we create in the course of our living are subjective or personal worlds that we create out of the given world. In an important way, however, this is an oversimplification. Both concepts of reality are true. The reality we create is from the point of view of Gestalt therapy as true as the one we "know" goes on without us. (In a way, the reality we create has an obviousness and immediacy that makes it seem more clearly true. We are intimate with the world we make; the independent existence of reality is a more abstract notion.)

The events of these two realities weave in and out of each other, acting and reacting upon each other. Reality is given, and we also create it according to our needs. The tension of these is the tension of a paradox, whose resolution is in the apprehension of experience as a unified process. Both given and created reality exist as gestalts for us, at different times, and each makes its contribution to the other and to the totality of our lives.

Excitement

Excitement in Gestalt therapy is used in a similar fashion to terms used in other philosophies and psychologies. It is Bergson's *elan vital*, Reich's orgone or sexual vegetative energy. It is Freud's libido (when that is seen as an animating force), and cathexis motion. It is Shaw's life-force. Excitement is the term used to refer to the manifestation of energy on our physiological and experiential levels. It refers to the animation of the organism. On the physical level, excitement is a function of the metabolism of the organism. It is the energy released and available to us from the activities we do to ensure our survival — finding food, breathing. As an undifferentiated form of organismic energy, it is referred to as general excitement. It is the energy of normal coping, of our sensory and motoric activities, of our thinking, of our life process. It is the form of our energy at our zero point.

Experientially, general excitement is felt as the undifferentiated feeling of being alive. This is the ground of phenomenological excitement. When the excitement of the organism flows into a coming gestalt, it is experienced as emotions. Emotions are the experiential correlates of organismic energy organized around the emerging gestalt formation. It is specific, focused excitement. Frustration, for example, is the experience of the tension of the organism or the environment resisting the demands of the need to form and carry through a gestalt. It is the experience of a rising excitement thwarted as it flows into the coming figure.

We are not stating a formula in which excitement makes the inert organism do something, like God's breath in a lump of clay. Excitement is an aspect of the relationship between the figure and the ground. It is not a force separate from the event that somehow makes it happen; excitement is not divisible from the parts of the organism/environment field. Nor is it simply a property of living things. In the process of creating and destroying a gestalt, the excitement of the field flows into the figure (which is usually composed of elements of both the organism and the environment). Excitement is a function of the figure, of the situation and its unfolding. Its phenomenological manifestations — emotions, the experience of energy and of being alive — come as well from that unification of the organism and its reality. This is different from the analytic idea of "cathecting the object." The Gestalt conception of excitement is an integrative one involving no objects; energy is part of the interaction of the aspects of the field.

The nature of free functioning in the field is that the aspects of the field are relating in a lively, constantly changing fashion. In this flux, excitement infuses all the parts of the process. A good analog to this is the way in which seeing depends on the movements of the eyes. The rods and cones of the retina ebb and flow in their excitation and contact with the visual field; and they scan it constantly, never resting at one place. Our eyes must move constantly in order to maintain contact; if we stare, we cease to see. In the same way, free-flowing excitement and contact are mobile and in flux, and these are characteristic of good functioning; conversely, if we stop the flow of excitement and movement that is our living process, we become dull and lifeless. The free-functioning organism is constantly readjusting and recontacting the environment. The interaction is always changing, a function of the free flow of excitement in it. Perspective changes, realities change, we change. Existence is this flux. Flowing with it, we remain contemporaneous.

Differentiation and the Dialectic of Polarities

At this time, we need to return to the process of organizing the field. We have seen that gestalt formation ends with the creation of a unified whole of meaning and activity that results in the gratification of the organism's needs. The beginning of this process is a different state of integration, the point of creative indifference. This is the zero point, *wu wei*, the beginning and the center. At this time, after satiation, we are open to the creative possibilities of the field, but not yet involved with them. Between these two states of functioning is a process of making the field clear and its different aspects distinct. This is necessary to the figure formation that comes after it; if we are to choose elements from the field to combine into coherent wholes, we must know what is available to us.

Differentiation is a process of separating the possibilities into opposites, into poles. We cannot be aware of distinctions without being aware of their polar nature. In this way, opposites are necessary to each other and closely related. Light is known in relation to darkness. Heat is known in relation to cold. Left is half the distinction of left and right. They are poles of distinction.

These dualisms pervade our behavior and understanding. We see ourselves as split into body and mind, our reality into the subjective and the objective. Our development is differentiated into biology and culture — nature and nurture — our expression into poetry and prose, work and play, our behavior into infantile and mature. Our emotions split into happy and sad, disappointed and satisfied; our morals into good and bad, our aesthetics into beautiful and ugly. Life is differentiated into ying and yang, form and emptiness, material and spiritual. Each of us divides our world into our likes and dislikes, friends and enemies, black and white, free and enslaved.

Polarities are deeply rooted in organismic functioning. Thirst leads to water seeking; being overheated leads to a search for a way to cool off. Being full of wastes leads to behavior to relieve ourselves of them. Gestalt formation is itself the organization of the field into the poles of figure and ground. These are biological phenomena, part of our self-regulation.

The relationship of the opposites is that the existence of one necessarily requires the existence of the other. This can be seen in the experiential relationship of the quantity and quality of sensations and emotions. When pleasure exceeds a certain point, it becomes unpleasant. The two are dynamically linked. This is reflected in ordinary language expressions such as, "Love is the first cousin to hatred," and "Opposites attract."

The interaction between polarities functions as a dialectical process. The opposites become distinguished and opposed; then, in their conflict, a resolution is achieved that unites the poles in a figure that is greater than the combination of the opposites — it is a new creation. The classic statement of this process is Hegel's conception of historical development as consisting of forces that form into a coherence called a thesis; the thesis is then opposed by the contradictions inherent in it, which cohere into its antithesis. The resolution of this conflict is a synthesis that transforms the opposing forces into a new and unified situation.

In dialectical thinking in Gestalt therapy, dualities are not irreconcilable contradictions, but distinctions that will be integrated in the process of gestalt formation and destruction. If the excitement present as the field differentiates is permitted to flow into the opposites, the result will be a resolution into a figural creation that is a genuine synthesis of them, and this will eventuate in a return to commonality and the undifferentiated field.

We can see from this that the more powerful the polarizations, the more significant the synthesis. "The greater the contrast," says Jung, "the greater is the potential. Great energy only comes from correspondingly great tensions between opposites." In every case, the possibilities are contained within the opposites. What is required is their interaction, so that the dialectic may be permitted to operate.

It is important to keep in mind that a dialectical understanding of the relationship between the different aspects of the field embraces the qualities that separate them and those that bring them together. Both the uniqueness and opposition of the elements of the organism/environment field and their inter-dependence and integration are stressed. The greatest cutting does not sever. Dialectical thinking is a holistic conception of dif-ferences.

We can restate the basic process of gestalt formation now, tak-ing into account the additional perspective that a knowledge of polarities and their interaction permits.

Taking as our starting point the zero point of the organism in its field, the field is undifferentiated. Our organismic needs are bal-anced; we are in a state of creative indifference. In the course of things, our zero point is disturbed by an alteration in the balance of the field. In the process of organismic self-regulation, aspects of the field begin to be distinguished according to the importance of their relationship to the needs of the organism. By the nature of that process, they are distinguished into polarities. The dynamic of the polarities is then unified into a figure that encompasses parts of the organism and parts of the environment in a unified whole of comprehension, and results in behavior that gratifies the need, destroys the figure, and restores the organism/environment bal-ance.

Said another way: I am working. I notice my lips are dry and I am thirsty; I begin to organize my field to obtain the water I want. I go to the kitchen, take a glass of water, and drink it. Refreshed and satisfied, I return to my work.

This step-by-step description is necessarily somewhat stilted, but when our functioning is free and we are in touch with our structures and processes, the actual event is a coordinated and graceful one. Fluid and unified behavior of this kind is a paradigm for natural healthy behavior in Gestalt therapy.

Chapter 3
HEALTH

*My miracle is that when I feel hungry,
I eat, and when I feel thirsty, I drink.*
ZEN MASTER BANKEI

In the preceding chapter we have seen that the basic principles of behavior in Gestalt therapy emanate from what has been called free functioning in nature. Free functioning, we said, is nature left to itself, flowing without second thought in the exigencies of the moment. What is natural is what is the normal occurrence in nature. Normal, natural, and healthy are different ways of saying the same thing.

Normal has different meanings. It can be used to refer to the majority of the events that we are interested in. "Everything is normal" — nothing unusual is happening. This is statistical normality.

Normal can also be used to mean what is desirable, or expected, or good. In this sense, we talk about norms of behavior, or we say (with a flavor of the first definition as well), "He certainly isn't acting like a normal person," i.e., he's acting strangely. Normal here is normative.

In free functioning, both these meanings are intended. Normality is both normative and statistical. Actually, it is the only thing that *can* happen in free-functioning organisms — the qualifiers are redundant. This is not the case when we speak of human events. What is statistically normal is far removed from free functioning in nature or the normal healthy processes of organisms left to themselves. "Normal" is what we all are, those of us who are not disturbed, or certified insane or neurotic.

In Gestalt therapy, the inspiration for a conception of what is normal and healthy does not come from the everyday lives most of us lead. "Normality," the experience we have of living in embattled America in the seventies, is a chronic state of disequilibrium in which the gratifications we seek never come. We live with a continuing low level of frustration, fear and longing. Our senses are bombarded well beyond what we might need to cause us to respond, yet we are dull and empty; our experience bats us over the head, but we are confused. We are full of questions about meaning and the worth of our existence, and our introspection brings us no relief.

What is normal about this is that it is epidemic. We are no different from most of our neighbors, though some are clearly worse off than we, it seems — they suffer more, and perhaps they cry out.

Normal in the context of this chapter is our integrated, healthy behavior. Though few of us attain normalcy as a regular way of being, all of us have our moments of single-minded, wholehearted activity. We know it in the lively and sometimes outrageous creative activities we occasionally find ourselves involved in, and in the spontaneity of young children. Perhaps each of us can recall moments — special moments we think of wistfully, with relish — when we have come alive and enjoyed our own absorption, our excitement, our joyousness. Moments like this occur in psychotherapy, and this experience of realigning the self, reintegrating neurotic structures and growing into new modes of behavior furnishes us with examples of normal, healthy behavior. These events and experiences and what we learn of processes in nature form the basis of the Gestalt understanding of healthy human behavior. This is the high side of normal, beyond mental health, instances of creative adjustment that exemplify the best of which we are capable. The Gestalt conception of health described in the following pages stems from these realizations of our best possibilities.

The advantages of defining health in this way are that it allows us a standard for appreciating and judging the quality of life as we live it and as we see it lived around us, and that we can have a perspective of possibilities that can serve as a challenge, a spur, and a hope to us. What we call neurotic behavior is neurotic because we have evidence that other modes of living are more suited to us, and more satisfying. It is less than our best effort. And understanding our present behavior in the context of our possibilities can support us as we try to grasp what we are capable of.

The Aspects of Health

First, healthy behavior in human beings must be integrated behavior. In health, we are at one with all our capabilities and the process that makes us up. We identify with all these vital functions. In health, we are not living an uneasy truce between the warring factions of our psyche, nor are we dominated by the dictates of our mind, our body, or our will. Holistic in functioning, all of our self is a part of our ongoing activity. It is not enough, for example, to be in touch with the sensory pleasure of eating. "Merely seeking to gratify the organ of taste without realizing when you have taken enough is called sensual eating," says Huang Po. Our stomach is also part of that activity, and ignoring it is not holistic behavior. This is the meaning of F. S. Perls' often-quoted description of "the real person who lost his mind and came to his senses" (F. S. Perls, undated, g). We don't function effectively by our minds alone, or by our senses alone.*

Integration is a prerequisite for the satisfactory functioning of figure/ground development. To create gestalts that will meet our needs, we must be able to choose from all our possibilities. If we cannot call on all the parts of ourself, our gestalts will be correspondingly weak. If our behavior is integrated, we have integrity. We are honest and authentic. We can be obliged to be cruel and unpleasant, but this is a necessary outgrowth of our honest behavior.

---

*Though he seems to be telling us to rely only on our sensations, Perls often sacrificed precision to the didactic demands of the situations he worked in. Much of his published work consists of transcripts of talks he gave to audiences who exemplify our cultural reliance on rationality and cognition. His purpose was to change his listeners, and he used words as ammunition, for effect.

Satisfactory formation and destruction of gestalts is, then, another aspect of our healthy behavior. In fact, in Gestalt therapy it is the functional definition of health. Since gestalt formation is the basic organismic function, the existence of clear, strong gestalts is the central criterion of health. The ability to form gestalts freely and appropriately means that the experience of living will have the depth and satisfaction that is health's hallmark. This criterion is autonomous, standing apart from and yet common to any particular realization of ourself. It is not necessary that we understand or work through all the problems and traumas that have accumulated in the course of our lifetime to be healthy, nor is it necessary to avoid making mistakes. The former is not always to the point of our present living, and mistakes are essential to health and growth. The ability to create and destroy gestalts, the process by which we live in tune with our abilities, is both a simpler and more apt definition of health. Health is possessing the ability to deal successfully with any situation we encounter now, and success is the satisfactory resolution of situations according to the dialectic of gestalt formation and destruction.

Working out gestalts in free functioning does not mean that no effort is involved. Health does not insure that obstacles topple when we meet them — it only means we apply ourselves to the task at hand with all we have. Nor is this spontaneous activity the same as doing anything we want to. It is doing what we want when we are centered — fully in touch with ourselves and the environment.

Out of the accumulation of these successes comes the confidence that we will prove to be adequate to circumstances. These successes are our support, and this support constitutes our security. We cannot be sure that everything will be all right all the time — we can never be sure of that, and trying to achieve it only interferes with what needs to be done. In fact, in the process of gestalt formation and destruction we may feel we are risking ourselves, but with repeated success we come to have confidence that we will deal with situations as they come, with the abilities we have; that their resolution will be as satisfactory as the situation permits, and that will be good enough.

Further aspects of health require that we know what we need. We must be in touch with what is important to us. To know what we need we must know and accept what we are at the present moment, for our needs are imbedded in our existence in the here-and-now. Implied in this requisite for good gestalt formation is its converse: we must know what we are not. Differentiating what is us and what is not, we can distinguish ourselves from the rest of the field. "If a man identifies with his forming self and alienates what is not organismically his own, he is healthy."

This is what Fritz Perls had in mind in formulating and encouraging the use of what he called "the Gestalt Prayer."

I am I and you are you
I am not in this world to live up to your expectations
And you are not in this world to live up to mine
I do my thing, and you do your thing
If by chance we should meet
It's beautiful
If not, it can't be helped.*

This is a central axiom of good functioning in Gestalt therapy. Only as all the elements of the field exist as distinct and separate entities can they be related in a meaningful fashion. Only as things are different can they be unified. In human interaction, a genuine encounter requires we be wholly and only ourself. If, for example, we are attracted to another person because we believe he has the intelligence we wish we had, we are not relating to the person before us, but to a conception we have of him. It may be true or it may not — as often as not, we will be mistaken — but what we are relating to is the wishes we have projected onto them. The other is not separate from us, but is an externalization of our own wish. We relate to ourself; in truth we are not related at all.

Of course, and again, healthy functioning requires that we give ourselves over to the process, to the working out of our needs in the field. We are not seeking victory, we do not desire control. The situation, of which we are a part, controls, and we give ourselves up to it. We do not behave according to a theory, we have no goals; we don't aspire to be "genital characters," or "integrated," or "responsible," for these conceptions, when they influence our behavior, are obstacles to our free functioning. It is in this vein that we are to understand Perls' statement, "Maturity is going from environmental support to self support" (Undated, d).

---

*Perls did not mean the "prayer" as a supplication. His intention was that it be repeated like a mantra, until its meaning filtered through our whole being. It is a reminder. Understood in this way, the Lord's Prayer is not the plea of impotent men beseeching God to do for them what they cannot do for themselves. It is us resolving that we try to fulfill our godliness as we know it.

Environmental support is essential to us; Perls is saying that our health is undermined when we underestimate our own resources to accomplish those ends that will benefit and gratify us. If we depend on other aspects of the field to do for us what we can do for ourselves, we impair the process of gestalt formation by diffusing the distinction between ourselves and the environment.

Integration involves more than accepting all our wishes, needs, behavior, and skills as part of us. It also requires that we know ourselves as part of the field. "In health, we are in touch with ourselves and with reality" (F. S. Perls, 1969b, p. 241). We must live in a creative adjustment with the outer world, in a harmonious relationship with the environment of which we are a part. We are not aliens. We are not lords of this dominion, masters of the dumb and passive natural world. Nor are we masters or slaves of each other — that is not the end of free interplay of men in society. We are creatures of the world, and fellow creatures together.

The final aspect of healthy functioning is awareness: simply to apprehend with the full scope of our senses the phenomenal world inside and outside us as it occurs. "This ability to see is health." As Gestalt formation requires the organization of the disparate and pertinent parts of the field, so it entails in that process our experiences of those parts; we can deal only with what we know. The process cannot go on without our participation in it; our participation consists of being in touch with the field and the emerging figure, because the process is in them. It is not separate from them, acting on them — it *is* them.

"Happy is the people," it is said, "who have no history." We carry the past with us as a burden if it still has a claim on us, and those of us who leave the past behind are rare. As the past appears in our living, it interferes with our present awareness. It becomes our present awareness, and the other events of the present prevent us from giving ourselves single-mindedly to the present. Healthy behavior requires the peace that comes from leaving history to itself, so that we can attend to what is happening to us now.

Awareness is a happening in the present moment. All we can be aware of is what is happening now. Even our reflections and reminiscences take place now, in the present. To understand with our whole being what "now" means is health. For if we are totally aware of now, we are in touch with all of what exists for us, and the process by which our living occurs issues from that. In the present are our needs and the means to bring them about as well as the situation now will permit. Living totally in the present is health; everything necessary for the best possible solution in the circumstances is here, now, in the circumstances.

A model of healthy functioning often cited in Gestalt therapy is the creative activity of the artist. As Otto Rank emphasized in his work, the creative act is psychological health. The psychology of art is the psychology of everything; it is a paradigm of mustering the materials of the field with spontaneous imagination, directness, awareness, and skill in the service of challenging and enlarging the self. Here, the cohesive organismic intelligence called intuition is at work.

This description of the artistic process is from the motion picture director Ingmar Bergman.

> The most important thing in the creative job is to let your intuition tell you what to do. I am writing a script and I plan for this man that he will do such and such. I know that if he does not do such and such, all these other things in the plot will fall into pieces. But my intuition tells me suddenly that this man says he will *not* do such and such. So I ask the intuition why. And the intuition says, I never tell you why. You have to find out for yourself.
>
> Then you go on a long, long safari in the jungle to follow where the intuition has directed. But if I refuse the intuition then I have merely arranged things. So my characters, they don't obey me. They go their own way. If they had to obey me, they would die.

We leave behind the safe structures we have been, leaping to a new way of dealing with the contacted field, engaging its possibilities. At the moment of achievement, we stand out of the way, giving in to the self-process.

Personality: The Self

Theories develop because we wish to understand something; theories of human behavior come out of our need to know ourselves and our wish to rid ourselves of the disabling elements of our lives. Perhaps if we know what is, we can know what is wrong, and what to do about it. Let us continue the Gestalt understanding of behavior by filling in the sketchy outline we have just concluded, and fitting the principles of behavior of the previous chapter more closely to the particular qualities of human beings.

When we speak of personality and its organization in Gestalt therapy, we refer to the figure of the individual as we know it over time. It changes in the course of our lifetime, and it is manifested differently in different situations, like a hand that is closed into a fist, and then open, giving; and then again curved around another hand. Any one of these by itself would be a deformed hand. All together, they are our hands in various contexts and different times. In the same way, we know and experience our personality as the disparate and yet unified sense of ourselves that continues throughout our lives. Holistically, the facets of the human personality are distinctions of a process that must be taken together. Often we can easily accept this; when behavior is spontaneous, and the circumstances favorable, the process of differentiation and integration flows smoothly.

The term in Gestalt therapy for the whole person is the self.* In total, you are yourself. The fundamental characteristic of the self is gestalt formation and destruction, what Freud called "the tendency to synthesis." The self is identical with those qualities of health enumerated above. The self is our essence; it is the process of evaluating the possibilities in the field, integrating them, and carrying them through to completion in the cause of the organism's needs. The self is the agent in contact with the present, carrying out the creative adjustment, making meaning. The self is our ongoing healthy processes, functioning for the existence and growth of the organism.

We know the self only as it is realized in the particular circumstances that involve it. In each situation, we are our self in touch with that situation. We are always our self, whether or not we are in touch with the present. We must be in touch with something. To actually realize our self, though, we must contact the actuality.

As situations vary, the manifestation of our self varies; it is always changing. Except for the specific expression of our self which is part of the present gestalt, we experience the self as a potentiality; or, from our experience, as a background.

Ideally, the character of the self in Gestalt therapy is stylistic.

---

*Gestalt therapy, as a development from psychoanalysis, uses some of the terminology devised by Freud and his followers. However, most of these terms — and especially the self, the id, and ego — are used in ways particular to Gestalt therapy. The reader is advised to put in abeyance any other uses of these terms with which he is familiar.

The self has a modality that is our particular way of being engaged in the process. It is our individual way of expressing our self in the contact with the environment. It stems from the results of our past growth and learning and their interaction with the individuality we bring into the world — heredity, constitution, karma. This realized self is like what is called Buddha-nature or mind in Zen. It is described in characteristic fashion. "This mind, which is without beginning is inborn and indestructible. It is not green or yellow, and has neither form nor appearance. It does not belong to the category of things that exist or do not exist, nor can it be thought of in terms of new or old. It is neither long nor short, large nor small, for it transcends all limits, measures, names, traces and comparisons. It is that which you see before you — begin to reason about it and you at once fall into error" (Huang Po).

The momentum of the self is to our complete involvement in the ongoing process of our living. The self works for its completion, for the making and finishing of gestalts. This is the realization of the self. The self is our involvement in any figure, even one that threatens us. Cooperation or conflict, a smooth or difficult process is the realization of self, because the process is happening and we are engaged in it. The self is us-in-process. It is the creating of the figure, not the figure itself. Its concern is the process, not our survival or security. The nearest we come to security is the belief that the process will eventuate in a resolution of the situation that satisfies the field.

The self, as it is understood in Gestalt therapy, is a unitary concept. It encompasses our physical, emotional, and cognitive aspects. Each of these are different manifestations of the activity of the self. Body, feelings, and brain are not separate, though they can be distinguished. For example, aspects of our cognition are, we know, functionally centered in our brain. But healthy intelligence is an organismic act; it involves not only our brain, but our brain and the rest of our behavior. Our thinking occurs in the context of the rest of our capabilities as a facet of the self.

At the point where the undifferentiated field begins to separate into discrete parts, boundaries emerge. These contact boundaries are points of difference, the point at which the self and the other meet. The boundary is not the point between the self and the other, it is of both parts, formed of their contact. In the same way, the boundary of the ocean and the coast is the lapping of the water on the shore; it is formed of both parts, and is not separate from it. Ebbing and flowing, it is both the line of demarcation and the point of connection. Our skins are contact boundaries. Separating our bodies from the environment, they are also our point of meeting with it. We sense the environment there, discovering what is us and what is not. The contact boundary forms as the self acts in the process of gestalt formation. Also called the awareness continuum, it is what we sense and what we think melted together.

The Aspects Of The Self

In the course of our functioning, the self has different qualities, or aspects, depending on the requirements of the situation and our ability to act in accord with them. Four aspects of the self are readily and regularly recognized: the id functions, the ego functions, the middle functions and the personality functions.

These dimensions of the self are called functions to emphasize the intimate tie between Gestalt theory and what we experience directly — the functions of the self are the different ways we experience ourself as we live our lives in contact with our environment. They are related to each other in the same way as are the facets of a jewel. Turned one way — in touch with one kind of situation — we see one side; turned another way, we see another. The self is the whole which these functions comprise. This whole is now totally only as an abstraction, in a kind of generalized present; we know directly, in the present moment, though, only the facets which are presently turned in our direction.

The self is experienced differently at different times because the system of contacts varies with the development of the figure, the requirements of the situation. (It amounts to the same thing.) Sometimes we feel ourselves as agents: we are doing, grappling, conceiving, willing (in the sense of "willful"). These are called the ego functions of the self, and the way it is put in Gestalt therapy is that the ego functions are the aspect of the self in which we feel ourselves as acting upon the environment. It is here we feel ourself to be responsible for our actions and making things happen. We chose, we deliberate, we decide, we insist, we impose, we manipulate — we make the figure.

Some of the ego functions are discriminative, actively dividing the field into elements which are part of the present gestalt — "identification" — and elements which are to be excluded from it — "alienation." Appropriately, the ego functions are expressed in English by the active voice. (Though some students of Gestalt therapy think that this aspect of the self, "taking responsibility" and "knowing what you want," is all there is to Gestalt therapy, we can see that they always have the ego functions facet of the self turned towards them.)

As we identify with what is of interest to us and disown for the moment what is uninteresting, we gain a clear sense of the difference between what is important to us and what is not, and a recognition of our ability to make these distinctions. Choosing what we identify with is experienced as the active imposition of ourselves on the environment. This description ought to be familiar to us. This willful, aggressive aspect of the self is a major element in our everyday awareness. For many of us, it is the predominant one. In part this is true because our culture values the ego functions for the way they manifest our "individuality."

When we are willing in that other sense, "I am willing to go along with that," the passive aspect of the self is recognized. When we are accommodating, when we feel moved, when we accept the qualities of the materials with which we are working, are sensitive to the atmosphere we find ourself in or harmonize with the tune we hear — these are the id functions. All feelings, for example, are experienced in this way. (It is implicit in, "I felt angry," that the feeling has come upon us. "I was moved," we say. Inauthentic, hysterical "feelings," the ones we manufacture, are the exception.) We use the passive voice to talk of these parts of ourselves.

In low levels of excitement, the id functions are free-floating, unstructured awareness and loose associations. An example is the state of semi-sleep where we are primarily aware of our bodily and mental processes going on, seemingly without us. We feel ourselves as acted upon and responsive to the environment, seemingly automatically. The id functions are that modality of the self where the vegetative functions and our native intuitions and impulses, with their special energy, excitement, and urge to movement are emphasized. Sometimes we experience it as being lost in the field or abandoned to our feelings, as when we cry unashamedly and wholeheartedly. Characteristically, our boundaries are felt only vaguely; sometimes they are not felt at all, and we feel ourselves at one with the processes of life.

In Gestalt therapy, playfulness, spontaneity, and full-throated expressions of emotions are considered necessary aspects of mature living. In health, they are id functions integrated into the ongoing functioning of the self. "Life is persistently more infantile than others, like Freud, allowed, and the absence of id functioning in 'mature' behavior is not a developmental change but the result of deliberate suppression that contributes to the neurosis of normality'' (Perls, Hefferline and Goodman, 1951, p. 436).

The id functions emphasize the integrated flow of free organismic excitement, to which we submit. In contrast, the ego functions emphasize aggressiveness, structure, and separation. The experiences of willfulness, struggle and effort are ego functions. But it does not follow that the ego functions necessarily predominate as the difficulties in the forming figure arise. There is more self, more sense of the hard work of figure formation, but adversity or complexity in figure formation coincides with increasing excitement, vigor and intensity as well as focus and intent. (Conversely, when figure formation is easygoing, there is perhaps a greater lightness and play, and diminished self.)

In our experience of the ego functions, coinciding with our sense of being forceful actors, is the feeling we have of being somewhat isolated from the field. We are separate entities, doing things to other things. Here is the root of our ability to objectify ourself or other things. Much of our higher thinking requires this frame of mind. It is our means of imposing distinctions on the field; and as we saw earlier, this perspective imbues the structure of our language. Similarly, many of our theories about nature and human events are based here. "Freud," said F.S. Perls, "never understood the self. He got stuck on the ego" (1969b, p. 11).

From the above, we can see that the id and ego functions seldom exist separately, without the other; rather, our behavior is usually composed of elements of both. In our experience, though, one or the other is foreground, at the center of our awareness. The relative importance of each depends on the activity in which we are engaged, our own personal style, and the phases of figure formation. Making love, for example requires more deliberation than sleeping and less than shopping — and some of us are more deliberate about lovemaking than others.

A third experience of ourself, and hence a third aspect of the self, is the middle functions, or middle mode, discussed earlier. It is the way we experience ourself when neither the active or passive aspects of the self dominate our experience. We are not in control, nor being controlled, but both, and neither, at the same time. It is the experience of participating in the figure as it develops, neither guiding it nor being guided by it, but doing our part. There is a middle voice or middle mode in many other languages — Greek, for instance — but not English. We express our awareness of the middle functions indirectly, as in, "I could not help but to...," or as I have in this paragraph. (Perls, Hefferline and Goodman therefore refer to the middle functions as the middle mode, as I did earlier. For consistency here, I use the former term.)

The combination of the ego and id functions which the middle functions seems to represent suggests a kind of polarity of the aspects of the self: the active ego functions against the passive id functions. While the balanced, synthetic quality of the middle functions supports this point of view, it is nonetheless a misleading one. First, it might suggest a rough analogy to the analytic opposition of id and superego mediated by the ego. But this analogy is not helpful at all. Besides the obvious difference between a Gestalt conception of a self of functional processes and an analytic one of psychic parts, the aspects of the self are not mediated by each other, as the id and superego are, by the ego. Rather, they are each mediated by the environment, by contacting, by the phases of figure formation and the elements of the field involved in it. It is more useful, less misleading, to consider the middle functions as a distinct kind of awareness, a distinct aspect of the self.

While we talk in Gestalt therapy of id and ego functions, there is no Id or Ego. Even when the id or ego are referred to, or capitalized, or called structures, it is clear from the context that the aspects of the self are ways of talking about our contact at different times. The Gestalt point of view avoids creating constancies, entities or reifications of these processes. The concepts are not mechanistic, but holistic. Even the self is thought of as the self functions, the systems of contacts at the present time. The constant here is the process of figure formation and destruction. Nothing is certain except change.

While there are no "parts" of "the self," we do of course have the experience of observing and recollecting ourself, and of drawing conclusions from our experience so that it seems to take on a more enduring quality. This book is an instance, as are any of our theories, stereotypes, characterizations, and summaries — anything which implies, "This is the kind of person (or thing or situation or world) I am." In Gestalt therapy, this is another of the aspects of the self, called the personality functions. They are the ways we can look at ourself and the ways we bring the past and future to bear on the present moment in the present moment.

We do it by remembering, anticipating, conceiving, by comparing our present and past experiences against a scheme of thought we have encountered or created. Here, we withdraw from the matter at hand partially or nearly totally to consider it or ourself, attending to our memories and systems of thinking, ordering the former according to the latter. We will, for instance, think about our own reactions to someone else, trying to make sense of them and us. So, among other things, it is the aspect of the self where we are aware of how we are taking apart and absorbing our experiences. That is, it is part of the initial stages of assimilation (the end of figure formation and destruction), tearing what has been experienced into palatable pieces; that is what taking thought is.

Yet, in spite of these important functions, it is said in Gestalt therapy that ideally, the self does not have much personality. In a system of thought which sees living as creative action in the world, it isn't hard to understand why, for the personality functions, bringing our mental processes to the fore of our awareness and comparing the present to past experiences and future possibilities, diminish the power and uniqueness of the present. It is not that we rule out considerations of the past or future in Gestalt therapy, but rather that the most sufficient figures come when figure formation is most lively, vigorous, free-ranging and coherent, and that in such times — most times — there is little of the aspect of the self which we call the personality functions.

We can see how the personality functions are akin to the rest of the gestalt concepts. They do not comprise personality, but are the experience of observing and considering and concluding. Our own conceptions, ideas of ourself and the world — personality, character — are the result of the personality functions. In health, we experience ourself in one or another of these dimensions of the self according to the phase of the figure. (Contrarily, it is a sign of unhealth that we are too much the same.) So, for example, in the beginnings of figure formation, the zero point and the first stirrings of excitation and figure/ground differentiation, our awareness is often of the id functions. Later on, putting things together and checking things out or struggling with materials or temptation, the ego functions tend to predominate. Still later, in the ripeness of full or final contact, our absorption is total. Since everything not related to the figure is so far in the background as to be absent from our awareness and it is usually too late for alternatives, our experience is not of a boundary with its meeting of differences, but only a unified figure — loving, working, crying, running. In this spontaneous time, our experience is of the middle functions. We can see from this that the self (and the sense of oneself) in Gestalt therapy is different at different times. Sometimes we are a do-er, sometimes we are the one being done to. Sometimes we have hardly any sense of ourself at all; we are inseparable from time and space and the events in which we participate. From this point of view, there is no enduring you (though you may think there is).

Contact and Support

The functioning of the self changes along two dimensions. The first dimension is style; the styles of the self are id and ego functioning. The second dimension is contact.

Contact refers literally to the nature and quality of the way we are in touch with ourselves, our environment, and the processes that relate them. Contact is seeing another's face; contact is experiencing and noting the texture of handwoven cloth, or the queasiness we feel when we eat too much. Good contact is being engaged fully in contacting, so that our absorption in what we are in touch with is thorough and satisfying. It is seeing another's face with immediacy, without a gray veil made of our expectations or opinions about what we are seeing, without the interference of our tiredness or boredom.

Poor contact coincides with our disinterestedness in what we encounter, or our fear of it, or the filter of our mentation or hang-ups. The depressed person to whom the world is dull and lifeless is in poor contact with himself and his world.

We have already seen that contact is an essential aspect of gestalt formation. Good figures require the comprehensiveness and excitement that characterize good contact. It is possible, in fact, to understand gestalt formation as the development of contact. Forecontact is the first stirrings of the figure and the division of the field into what is in and out of it. This segues into the later stage of contacting, where the figure is coming clear and our contact is more focused and precise. Final contact is the resolution into a figural whole, and the solution of the problem that called forth the gestalt; and postcontact is the process of gestalt destruction and the return to a point of balance.

Healthy contact is not fixed, but mobile. We feel out what we are contacting, we don't hang on to it. We alternate contact and withdrawal, going from one to the other and back again in the same way we alternate waking and sleep. This flowing process is a basic rhythm of healthy functioning.

Part of the flux of contact comes from its experimental nature. The formation of gestalts, especially in its beginning and intermediate points, is not a smooth or infallible process. It proceeds often by fits and starts, the figure forming, dissolving, and reforming again as we become aware that the choices we are making are not quite the best ones for the situation. Contact and engagement ebb and flow in this process of trial and error. Mistakes are an inevitable part of healthy functioning. They are part of our finding the creative invention that is most apt for the unique situation we are in. Errors are more accurately understood as part of our playing with the elements of the field as we go about finding the best adjustment we can manage.

Contact depends on what we call the support functions of the organism/environment field. If contact is the figure of healthy functioning in the field, support is the ground. Seeing a friend's face, we note his Wedgewood blue eyes, his willingness to look at us as we look at him, the wrinkles along his mouth and nose, the stubble on his chin. We are in touch with his appearance, and we are also in touch with feelings he conveys to us — warmth, fatigue, openness. We are also aware of our own participation in the interaction: our caring for him, our pleasure in being with him.

The support for our contact in this situation is manifold. Most immediately, it is the acuity of our vision, our willingness to be intimate, and our ability to experience and understand our perceptions and feelings. More generally, our breathing supports us, feeding our excitement and our metabolism supports our body; our body holds us up, supporting us literally. Ultimately, this system of supports for this single activity extends out to the limits of the universe: to the air we breathe and the food we eat, thence to all the other animate and inanimate things that contribute to the ecosystem we inhabit. It extends back in time as well to our ancestral supports, our generic heredity, to our development as human beings on this earth, to our karmic affinities and predispositions, and eventually to the first cause.

Our support, then, comes from our physiology, posture, coordination, from the sensitivity of our orienting faculties and our motoric skills. It comes from our ability to use language to articulate our needs and responses, and from our self-knowledge — our ability to be in touch with our present feelings and thoughts.

The particular qualities of our support come from the same source as our contacts: from our heredity and constitution, and from the results of previous gestalts and their resolution. Our present support depends on the success we have had in the past in carrying through the process of creating and destroying gestalts, for these past successes give us the confidence to let the process carry us on.

Support also comes from the rest of the field, from the air we breathe and the food we eat and from the social conditions of which we are a part. We flourish when we have what we need. The basic elements we require are love and acceptance, and the physical, emotional, and intellectual stimulation that allows us to exercise all our abilities. These are the support required for healthy contact, and thus for successful gestalt formation.

Awareness, the Present

Another part of the contact dimension of the self is awareness. To be in touch with the emerging gestalt means to be aware of the field. Healthy functioning requires that we contact the figural elements and that this contact registers with us. Good contact requires consciousness. If we are not aware of the contact, our behavior will be either randomly or persistently inappropriate; the demands of the situation change as they develop and our preconceptions cannot keep pace with the uniqueness of each gestalt. Consequently, our opportunities are realized only partially, and both the solution and our self-gratification suffer.

To be aware, we must have empty heads. There is an old story:

Nan-in, a Japanese master during the Meiji era (1868-1912) received a university professor who came to inquire about Zen.

Nan-in served tea. He poured his visitor's cup full, and then kept on pouring.

The professor watched the overflow until he no longer could restrain himself. "It is overfull. No more will go in!"

"Like this cup," Nan-in said, "you are full of your own opinions and speculations. How can I show you Zen unless you first empty your cup?"

(Reps, 1957, p. 19)

To be empty is to be open to the possibilities. This ensures that whatever gestalt develops will be able to draw on all the pertinent aspects of the field. Once we begin to judge, we can no longer allow the gestalt to emerge freely. Our thoughts and opinions about what we experience interfere with the experience itself, narrowing the possibilities. To the extent we limit ourselves in this way, the gestalts we form are likely to be weak and inept, and our experience will correspondingly be colorless. Authentic behavior comes only when the figure is drawn from what we freely prefer. This is F. S. Perls' point in "The most creative, richest person has no character" (1969z, p. 7). Character is inflexibility.

This is the concept of creative indifference, the organism at its zero point, open to what will come. This is what Perls has referred to as "the fertile void." It is an emptiness full of potentiality, awaiting the inevitable disequilibrium. If we are aware of it, it will dissolve as the needs of the situation appear. If we attend to it, we maintain the vitality of our experience. If we do not, we miss our chances. Having that much less to experience, we commensurately have that much less satisfaction. "Be open, even to emptiness," says Ingmar Bergman, "because then whatever does come will be real."

To be aware is to be responsible. In Gestalt therapy, this word is used in two ways. First, we are responsible if we are aware of what is happening to us. To take responsibility means, in part, to embrace our existence as it occurs. The other and related meaning of responsibility is that we own up to our acts, impulses, and feelings. We identify with them, accepting all of what we do as ours.

These are distinct and different meanings. We are responsible for things we clearly *do* — for being angry, or obstinate, or irresponsible; for breaking dishes and giving gifts. We are responsible as well for the injuries inflicted on us, and the presents we receive, for what is done to us. Here we are responsible for our part in the event — for the pain we feel and the taking of the gift. When it rains, we get wet. While we didn't make it rain, we are responsible for being wet. We are also responsible for our middle mode experiences, for the things we participate in and give ourselves up to. We do not make ourselves love, or hate, but they are the feelings we have. We are responsible for having those feelings, not because we caused them to be, but because they are our existence at this moment.

In healthy functioning, these aspects of responsibility alter with the quality of the functioning of the self. In aspects of ego functioning, we are more aware that we *do* something, or have it done to us; in id functioning, our experience is usually middle mode. In the flow of the self, they fuse together and separate out as the situation dictates, against the ground of awareness and responsibility that is our sense of living our lives.

(Responsibility has another meaning in ordinary usage, of obligation. We are responsible in this sense if we do what is expected of us and what we have committed ourselves to. In healthy functioning in a tolerable environment, this is not different from the above, but normally it often involves doing things we dislike or resent because we feel we ought to. In Gestalt therapy, this kind of responsibility is considered irresponsible because it neglects our needs and the spontaneous working out of gestalt formation in favor of functioning by self-imposed regulations.)

There is only present awareness. Contact and support require our awareness if they are to weigh in healthy functioning. Awareness in turn is the experience of what is in front of us now. Contact, experience, and change are all possible only in the present. We can be aware of things that happened in the past or will (we hope, or fear) happen in the future, but our awareness is happening now. We must live in the present, we have no choice. "This ever-changing something, elusive and unsubstantial, is the only existing reality."

This does not mean that nothing has ever happened before now, or that there is no future, nor does it mean that events have no origins and no direction. It means that at this moment, we are here, not there. Being oriented to the past or future is an occurrence in the present moment, and these other occurrences take their bearings from the present moment; they derive their meaning from the present. We recall or anticipate in the context of our present existence. The past and future exist in us, dependent on us for their life. They are part of the unity of our present existence. "Beginningless time and the present moment are the same. There is no this and no that."

While we cannot help but live in the present, we all know it is possible for us to direct most of our attention away from it. Natural behavior, however, is present-centered. In health, our awareness is of the present moment, of the present process of gestalt formation. We live the life that is before us now.

It is impossible to overemphasize the importance of the awareness of the present in Gestalt therapy. To be in the present, "in the now," brings into being all the other aspects of healthy functioning. Being in the present ensures the existence of the figure/ground process in all its aspects. To be here, now, means to allow that process to come about and work itself (and us) through.

Living in the present is its own reward. Our experience in the present is the working out of our gratifications and the needs of the field in which we participate. We work and play for the sake of the work and play. Gratifications are not deferred; they exist in the process and in the outcome. We are gratified in the experience of working out our needs as well as in the solution. In the same way, the satisfaction of our eating is not only in filling our stomachs; it is also in the experience of contacting our hunger, finding what will satisfy it, in biting, chewing, and dissolving the food, in swallowing it. Actually, our satisfaction emanates from our involvement in these processes and consists of being thoroughly engaged in them. It is not separate from these activities; experiencing our existence is its own fulfillment.

Health in Society

The implication of the preceding sections of this chapter for political and social philosophy is that we are at our best in circumstances where free functioning and the lively interplay of individuals and the environment is permitted. The kind of social order that makes possible the most adequate solutions to the problems of living comes out of free functioning; it cannot be imposed in advance of the fact of a problem by social and political structures.

As a political philosophy, this is Anarchism. With a small *a*, anarchy is akin to chaos — "mere anarchy," in Yeats' phrase. But with a capital *A*, Anarchy is free functioning in society, people left to structure their lives and interactions to meet the needs of the field. From the anarchist perspective, anything but Anarchy is chaos. Order — the imposition of structure on an event from outside it — is chaos since it impedes free functioning. The result of order must be chaos since only the unhindered attempts of men can produce adequate solutions. Anything less than adequacy will lead to chaos. In order for us to work out the strivings of our selves, the environment must provide a tolerable background within which we can do the things that are important to us. These cannot be done for us by the social order, but it can prevent them from happening by laying structures and conventions on the social fabric that hampers free functioning.

The alert, ongoing, everchanging give and take of the social situation results in justice. The interaction of surplus and deficit in human relations allows all the parties to the process to achieve a realistic and satisfactory balance for themselves. Taken a step further, Anarchy is a way of living that includes all the elements of nature in its interplay. The give and take is an exchange between men, and between men and the ecological network that we are imbeded in. All living creatures and the inorganic elements of the universe together constitute the field, and our free functioning requires that we maintain contact with all the field and include it in the series of creative adjustments that make up the quality of our lives on this planet.

Obviously the conditions of life do not always permit us to move freely to satisfy our needs. When that is not possible, the results are not as good. To the extent that the solutions we make are impoverished by restrictions on the materials we can incorporate into them or by rigidities in the process itself, we live in impoverished circumstances.

It might seem from the foregoing that Gestalt therapy ties our individual health and satisfaction to the health and satisfaction of the society in which we live. In a way, this is true — any misfortune affects us all. There is a strong emphasis in the Gestalt writings on the importance of benign surroundings, which is reflected in the preceding discussion. In its most obvious sense, this point is beyond argument: health is likely to be better in a supportive situation than in a concentration camp, and our creative adjustments will satisfy us to the extent that we are left to our own devices and to the extent that materials to make these adjustments are present.

At the same time, this emphasis is not construed in Gestalt therapy as necessarily correlating social health and personal health. We are not dependent on the grace of institutions for our health. We may function well in conditions of adversity and scarcity as well as of plenty. Health is not equivalent to happiness, surfeit, or success. It is foremost a matter of being wholly at one with whatever circumstances we find ourselves in. Even our death is a healthy event if we fully embrace the fact of our dying. (At that point, what choice do any of us have?) The issue is awareness, of living in the present. Whatever our present existence consists of, if we are at one with it, we are healthy.

The Unconscious and Gestalt Therapy

Gestaltists do not use the concept of the unconscious in their work, nor does it play a part in their theorizing. This attitude is a principled one, springing from the foundations of the Gestalt approach and arising in response to ideas and practices of other therapeutic schools.

From the point of view of Gestalt therapy, the concept of the unconscious is inimical to good therapeutic work, sound psychological thinking, and healthy functioning. First, understanding our behavior in terms of conscious activity and behavior motivated by the unconscious is a fragmented way of understanding ourselves. It stands opposed to the Gestalt emphasis on wholeness and unity. This theoretical split between conscious and unconscious behavior implies a host of other divisions, between fantasy and reality, between what is inside us and what is outside us, between our interior processes and our behavior.

Now, in Gestalt therapy we do not say that these are not different; but, if our model of human functioning states that we have an everyday conscious self and — somewhere within us — an unconscious self, we underline these differences and make them irreconcilable, because we are saying that the structure of our psyche is divided. From the Gestalt point of view, this is a reification, making a state of affairs into an irreversible fact. It assumes that man is permanently split, by nature.

We are not denying the experience of this split. In "normal," neurotic life, this experience of fragmentation is a frequent one. But Gestalt therapy does not use this kind of normalcy as its standard of health. The notion of an unconscious is largely rooted in our confusing health with "normal" behavior. In neurotic functioning, we are out of touch with many of our needs, skills, and feelings. Hence we often find we are doing and thinking things that surprise us. This is the experience that forms the basis of most of the theory of the unconscious in traditional psychology.

In Gestalt therapy, we emphasize the achievement of unified functioning. This is a dynamic process that alternates polarization and unification; by contract, the concept of the unconscious is a static one, and the state is one of permanent dichotomy.

Instead, Gestaltists speak of awareness and lack of awareness. In the formation of gestalts, for example, what does not become figure may momentarily be lost to our consciousness: in pursuing an argument, we are unaware of our thirst or hunger. The contents of the unconscious are out of our awareness, either because they are irrelevant to the present course of our living, or because we actively keep aspects of ourself out of our awareness.

This approach allows us to integrate our needs, our dreams, our fantasies, and our creations into our daily lives. They are not artifacts of the domain of the dark region of our soul that have to be subjugated to the willful, deliberate activities of ego mode functioning, with its preponderance of rationality, introspection, and verbalization. Instead, the task of therapy is to organize and unify and integrate all these into our functioning. In the Gestalt conception of healthy functioning, aspects of the self move in and out of awareness as they are necessary to the circumstances. We are not moved by unconscious wishes but by organismic self-regulation as it is expressed in the ongoing situation.

The Gestalt approach takes us away from the inevitable accompaniment of focusing on the conscious/unconscious split — speculating about things we do not experience. It points us instead toward the present — toward our behavior, our experience, and the interplay between us and our environment. What is happening right now *is* what is really going on.

Jung's formulation of the unconscious resembles the Gestalt formulation of the development of awareness of the self in some important ways. Both emphasize the existence of an untapped potential within us that is filled with possibilities for new growth and self-realization, and both urge the integration of what we know about ourselves and what we don't know. By contrast with other notions that underscore only the murky, alien, and dangerous aspects of the parts of ourselves we don't know about, this is a more accurate (and also more optimistic) conception.

Health, Growth, Learning, Maturity: Centeredness

Health, we have seen, is the integration of the organism and the environment through creative adjustments that come about by the formulation and destruction of gestalts. Inner conflicts, and conflicts between our social and personal needs, are compatible with healthy functioning. What is required for health is our continuing creativity in these circumstances. To be able to stay with the obstacles and carry out the situation into one that satisfies us is health. No other norms are necessary.

This is, in a way, a process of continually befriending aspects of the field. As we are involved in the coming figure and its resolution, we put parts of ourselves in an interaction with other parts of the field — other people, plants, animals, objects. In this interaction, they are inside our self-boundaries. We are identified with them. Our relationship to them is no longer (in Buber's terms) one of I and It; it becomes one of I and Thou. In this way, we assimilate the field, changing it by changing our relation to it.

Growth goes on in this way. We are continually reorganizing ourselves and our relationship to the environment. We must do this if we are to live, for healthy living is a process of creative adjustments.

To be able to be grounded in this process and live with it is maturity. In Gestalt therapy, it is called being centered. Simply, to be centered is to deal with the circumstances of our lives as they present themselves according to the dictates of healthy functioning outlined above. Centered, we freely engage in the process of change that is free functioning. We are responsible for our existence. We are ripe. We have achieved that state of being that our structure will come to if we and the environment permit. We are not submissive to the demands of society nor defiant of them; neither are we self-effacing or self-aggrandizing. Centered, we are in touch with and controlled by the situation. Our teleology has run itself out, and we are what we are capable of.

Notice that the particular form of maturity is not spelled out. It cannot be. Vested in the unique occurrences of our lives, our maturity takes the form of our self functioning in our reality. For each of us, living in unique social, cultural, and personal circumstances, maturity will be different. What is the same is our engagement in those differing situations. Whatever it is, we will be all there.

That is the macrocosm of growth. Its microcosm is the conclusion of one gestalt. Growth is not an instantaneous achievement. It goes forward incrementally, often with pain and suffering, but in any case one gestalt at a time.

In the midst of making a figure, we do not know what will transpire. We know what is in front of us, and we know what has been in the past, but in creating the gestalt, we must give ourselves to the process. We must take a risk. To grow, to invent the new way the new situation requires, we must take a chance.

Concluding the Process

The arrival of the gestalt is the creation of knowledge. It is the making of the truth suited to the particular situation. This is learning, growing, discovering; it is making personal knowledge apt and useful. In this act, we learn to rely on our own talents. "When we discover, we uncover our own ability, our own eyes, in order to find our potential, to see what is going on, to discover how we can enlarge our lives, to find means at our disposal that will let us cope with a difficult situation" (F. S. Perls, 1970b, p. 18). We have gained the new ground of a solution we have made. We have learned to look to ourself for our gratifications. We are not independent, but we are not helpless, either. We have what it takes.

In Gestalt psychology, the reinterpretation of polarities is called the "Aha" experience. It is a moment of creative revelation. At this moment, we have changed the structure of ourselves and our environment and we will behave and think differently, because the field is new. We have reorganized it. This is not intellection only; that may not come until later, if at all. It is a total organismic change. We are new, and the old difficulty has been replaced by new behavior, a new us, a new world.

For a time, we may repeat the new solution, getting it into our bones until we have thoroughly mastered it. This is digesting the gestalt; in this way we make it familiar to us, allowing the reorganization that has occurred to affect every part of our being. We see this often in the development of children. Having found a new way to pile blocks on top of each other, they will return to the situation again and again, carefully working out their invention in the same way, until they are satisfied.

The new gestalt reverberates in us like a rock falling in a pond. As we become accustomed to it and the larger ripples die, it evolves into a feeling of peace, the experience of our satisfaction. The business of our lives that has taken so much attention is concluded. Writ large, this is the moment of orgasm turned to blissful quiet and sleep. Or it is the echo of music paling into quietude. We come, again, to the point of balance.

This is closure and satisfaction. As it passes, it falls away from the center of our interest. It had loomed large to us, now it recedes. The poles of figure and ground dissolve into the field.

In the peace of closure, we are not victorious. We may have gained a victory in accomplishing what we struggled for, but there are no victims. Our satisfaction comes in the flush of the new reality, not in standing over the ghosts of the past. Even in the heat of competition, our pleasure in winning is in mastering our capabilities and giving our all, and finding that was sufficient.

Peace may come as well with defeat. We have found our limits, and we know we have done all we can. In the striving to gain what we cannot have, in desperation and perhaps in rage, we give up our need for the impossible. The most obvious example of this is the mourning labor, working out our understanding that someone we have been close to does not exist anymore.

We have seen throughout that our emotions are formed as part of the excitement of the interplay of gestalt formation. And we see now that they come to fruition and release at the point of closure. Our emotions are part of the mobilization of the functioning of the self into the figure. They are created as part of our striving to relate aspects of the field in a meaningful way. We do not discharge energy randomly; we focus our excitement in the present context, and the resultant figure has as its emotional manifestation the pleasure or pain or anger or orgasm appropriate to the context. In healthy functioning, our emotions are coherent, essential aspects of our behavior that mobilize us to do the things we need to do. And as the figure/ground process draws to its end, our experience of satisfaction tells us that we have resolved the pressing problem that required our attention.

The argument here is with psychoanalysis, with Reich and his followers — Lowen, for example — with advocates of "rage reduction" and primal screams, and others who encourage catharsis and random expressions of emotions. Psychoanalytic writers tend to view strong expressions of emotion as "acting out," or else as unfortunate but necessary results of our animal natures. Here, sex and aggression are accumulations to be ventilated or discharged or sublimated. Reich, Lowen, Saslow, Janov, and many body therapists also share this bias, though their therapies encourage the discharge of emotions. In both cases, emotions are taken out of their relationships to situations of living.

Characteristics of Contact

The self has characteristic ways of making contact in the process of growth. In the forms described here they are aspects of health. Later we shall see how the same processes can operate as part of impaired and unhealthy functioning.

When we are at our zero point, prior to and after gestalt formation, our experience is of loose undifferentiated contact with the field. We may feel we are as much a part of our surroundings as we are of ourselves. We may experience a loss of our distinctness as we appreciate the stillness of the night or the rolling of the ocean waves. In this state, primarily a matter of our id mode functioning, we may feel we have become those waves.

At such a time, we say we are confluent with what we are in touch with. Our boundaries have become permeable and we appreciate the similarity of what we contact and ourself. Confluence is the appreciation of sameness. It is the kind of contact in which little or no contact is felt. Instead, we experience our empathy with our surroundings. At such times, if we are with another person, we may feel we truly understand his experience because we seem to be having it, even as he does.

Confluence is a major component in religious experiences of oneness, and it is the dynamic at work in certain drug experiences. This quality of sympathetic resonance that comes from maintaining contact with another at certain times is also the basis for the knowledge and intimacy we have with others. It is the bridge from man to man. The privacy of our isolated self is gone; instead, we allow another to share our experience, to know us. At this point of meeting, the contact is so true and we are so compatible that we feel the experience of another's existence.

Another normal contact characteristic with similarities to confluence is projection. In projection we also seem to dismantle the boundary of our self, but instead of taking the existence of the other into ourselves or merging with him, we put our existence into the other. The other — person or object — serves as a movie screen onto which we put an aspect of ourself. In normal functioning, this is the fantasy process by which we visualize the environment in a different form from that it presently has, in order to test out ideas for remaking the field. An architect, viewing a wooded hillside, projects a country house onto it. Looking in a mirror, we project a mustache on our clean-shaven face, or long hair on our short hair. Along the way of creating a gestalt to meet a present need, we avail ourself of our ability to see reality different from its actuality, more in accord with our desires. Or perhaps we rearrange aspects of the field in a different way from their present arrangement: thinking about how to reorganize the living-room furniture, or packing the car trunk. This process is the beginning of our invention itself. Abstracting the field and recasting it according to our needs, we can make art, or scientific discoveries. This activity is central to all creative thought, scientific, artistic, and practical.

In health, we eventually regain responsibility for our needs, and for what we have done. An example of this is the artist who makes over his reality to suit his muse. He enriches himself and his work by the interaction of the world and his fantasy of it, and he is responsible to both. He knows what is his fantasy and what is outside him. Healthy projection is circular in this way. Identifying the other with our needs or inventing them with our needs, we create a fantasy full of meaning. Though we may obliterate the actual other in the course of our invention — and even prefer what we have made to what we started with — we do not believe that our projections reflect the state of the field.

The developmental precursor of projection and confluence is the undifferentiated state of the infant. Boundaries are not yet well developed, the self functions primarily in the modality of the id. The infant has no concept of self and other, so there can be no boundaries. His environment is part of him, confluent with him.

Healthy introjection is similar to confluence but is stylistically linked more closely to the mode of functioning we have called ego than is confluence. It is clearer, and more forceful. Introjection is taking on attitudes and behaviors without the process of gestalt formation. It is rote learning, without assimilation. In introjected behavior, all we can do is play roles, because we have not become what we are doing. The gestalt that is us has not been altered by including the new material in it. We take on introjections like we put on a mask.

Healthy introjection is role playing that is known to be so. It is the play acting of a child or of an actor. In this way, we expand our possibilities, trying on new ways of being to see if they fit, or if we are interested in taking them in, or making them familiar and hence less threatening. (F. S. Perls uses the example of a child who goes to the dentist, has the usual painful experience, and plays dentist after she comes home. She is trying to gain some mastery in this fearful situation by taking the dentist's role.)

In introjection, there is a felt boundary, since introjection requires that the self functions predominantly in the mode of ego, separating out from the field the parts of it we introject. We know there is some difference between what we are and what we are doing.

Imitation, copying, and role playing are healthy introjection. In health, we discard them when we are done playing with them, or they become the initial aspects of figure/ground formation and in that way start to become real parts of us. Occasionally, as in the case of social conventions like shaking hands and saying "How are you?", the pervasiveness of the introject and the demand placed on us to take it in results in our taking in a part of the environment without assimilating it. But if they don't matter much to us, they slip by without difficulty as we accommodate ourself to our social reality.

Healthy retroflection is the self in the mode of ego ordering and regimenting our behavior according to the demands of the situation. It is what is called self-control. In healthy retroflection we control ourselves by an effort of will, forcing our energies into precise channels perhaps different from the ones they would take without retroflection. Good examples of healthy retroflection are learning to type, or learning to play a musical instrument. It is only with careful dedication and increasing control and refinement of our actions that we come to be able to do what we wish to do. The process of refining is retroflection. This is self-restraint under the auspices of the growth of the self. Healthy retroflection is discipline.

The Safety Functions

Another aspect of the self that is integral to health and important in understanding impaired functioning is the safety functions. In many ways, our abilities are remarkable and effective. Because of them, though, and because of adversity that cannot be surmounted, our skills lead to adventures where we find ourselves in trouble. From danger, or deprivation, or illness, we cannot find a way through to equilibrium. Our safety functions operate at this point to protect us and allow us to exhaust the energy that has gone into the aborted figure.

The most obvious safety function is flight. In an intolerable situation, we leave the scene. Another is desensitization — psychic flight. Faced with a situation where closure is not possible, we close down our orienting faculties, blotting out the contact by a process of motoric retroflection. We inhibit our awareness and suppress our responses; falling into sleep, or shock, or unconsciousness if the situation is difficult enough. In milder cases, we may just tune out.

What is called regression is also a safety function. Regression is reorganizing the organism/environment field so we can cope with it. We turn to other styles of behavior that can cope with it. We turn to other styles of behavior that gave us the support we need to deal with the situation at hand. Regression is the self operating to find a way of making the field tractable so a solution can be found. Hallucinations and delusions serve the same purpose. Here we use the ability to fantasize a solution that was remarked on earlier, and we place the fantasy at our contact boundary so that it replaces the unworkable situation. It is another kind of psychic flight.

This kind of solution does not, of course, deal with the situation, but it permits us to dissipate the excitement that has accumulated and that cannot otherwise find expression. It is cathartic. Our dreams regularly serve the same purpose. They permit us to be in a situation where we are supported — sleep — and to work off some of the energy generated by our unfinished business.

Consciousness, by itself, can serve a safety function. When the situation is unworkable but we are not obliged or able to leave it, contact can be used to exhaust the tension of the unfinished gestalt. Because no activity can come from it, the impetus to figure formation dissolves as we stay in contact with the situation.

All these safety functions are in themselves healthy — that is, they are part of our being and can be used in the service of our health and growth, in our best interests. They also play a large role in organismic disorders, as we shall see, where they become a persistent mode of organismic functioning. When the self continues to operate in any of these ways in the absence of the circumstances that occasioned them, they are chronic and inappropriate, and hence aspects of impaired functioning. Even so, their roots are in the tendency of the self to make the best possible solution in the field.

In free functioning, we live our life to the extent of its possibilities. "That which is before you is it, in all its fullness, utterly complete," says Zen master Huang Po. In the give and take of our existence, even our failures satisfy. We do not raise questions about the meaning or worth of our living, or the point of the suffering we experience and see around us.

"Questions like...what is life's meaning, are not meaningful. I come to them when, attempting to be quiet and at ease, I consult my memories and my plans instead of giving way to the cries of anger and pain that would otherwise overwhelm me" (Goodman, 1968a, p. 45). Living, we have no need to ask for meaning. Our questioning interferes with our awareness of our present existence; replacing the flow of the dialectic with preconceptions, we are dissatisfied. So, we ask for the grand formulae: What am I living? What is the point of life? Why do we die and suffer?

Living spontaneously, we do not think to ask. We live in the ripeness of each moment. Our activities have direction and import, and our experience suffices for our satisfaction. We live, as Kant said, with a sense of purpose, without a purpose.

Chapter 4
ABNORMAL
FUNCTIONING

Neurosis is the avoidance of legitimate suffering.
C. G. JUNG

With one behind you cannot sit on two horses.
ROMANI (GYPSY) SAYING

It is impossible to examine the variety of human enterprises and the ingenuity of our solutions to life's problems without being impressed with the genius of which we are capable. The history of civilization is replete with heroic adventures, and admirable creations from the earliest records of man's tenure on this earth to the present day punctuate the record of our existence. Nor is it only the especially gifted and fortunate among us who have attained these heights. On occasions of intimacy, in the satisfaction of a good job well done, in the siren of crisis we recognize the fruition of the same impulses in the common man.

Moreover, we have seen that our very being provides the resources for continuing to construct fruitful and rewarding styles of living. We are made so that we can realize the possibilities of the resources within and without us. Indeed, the force of the impulses described earlier and the instances of their realization that we know of make it remarkable and even unbelievable that we are, many of us, often so unhappy.

We do ourself no service to presume that the widespread dissatisfaction and misery surrounding us is an unsolvable mystery, or an aberration. The same record of history and the experience of people are of endless wars, pointless tragedies, empty and wasted lives, and mutual and self-disparagement. "Our misery," notes Goodman (1968a, p. 141), "seems so ingrained that it calls for an explanation from our essential natures."

Any understanding of man that will touch his essential being must entail all the facts of his existence in it if it is to be adequate and useful. We must be able to appreciate limited, impaired, and disappointing lives as emanating from our selves, our natures, as clearly as we recognize and approve of the experiences that ennoble us. It will not do to look upon the fabric of our everyday dilemmas as being woven from a different warp and woof from our best moments; nor can we fail to come to grips with it at all, regarding it as accidental, or darkly fortuitous.

Much of what we know to be our despair, frustration, and unhappiness is called mental illness, neurosis, psychosis, disorders of character and behavior. Much of the remainder is "normalcy," an epidemic, unhealthy response to our circumstances that "...perhaps has a viable social future" (Goodman, 1968b, p. 83). These are all as basic to us as anything else we are or do.

The Fall of Man

In every religion, and in every psychology, there is a version of man's fall from grace. The most familiar to us is the story of Adam and Eve in the Garden of Eden, but every civilization and culture have made their own, to answer the question: How did we fall into this?

In Buddhism and Hinduism, man's fall stems from the ego, his separation from the ground of being, from mistaking the distinctions that he perceives for the whole picture of himself and ignoring his partnership in the universe. Freud's origin of the fall was based on his understanding of the interaction of parents and children as necessarily difficult and commonly tragic.

A version of all the fall of man can be found in the literature of Gestalt therapy, too, in the form of an interpretation of the Old Testament story of Adam and Eve (Goodman, 1968a). The biblical story, we remember, is: After God had made the world, he made a garden in Eden, and put Adam, the man he had made, in it. In the garden were trees both good to the sight and abundant with food, and also two special trees: the tree of life and the tree of the knowledge of good and evil. God forbade Adam to eat the fruit of the last-named tree; if he did, he would die. Then God brought the creatures He had made to Adam, and Adam named them.

Then God made Eve. Anon, the serpent in the garden convinced her to eat of the fruit of the tree of knowledge of good and evil; he said, rightly, that it would open her eyes and make her like God, knowing good and evil. She did, and Adam did as well when she offered some to him. They did not die from their repast; instead, they realized their naked state, and clothed themselves.

It was obvious to God that they had eaten the forbidden fruit. Saying He did not want Adam to take the fruit of the tree of life as well and live forever, God drove him out of Eden, and He set a flaming sword at its gate to guard it. (We assume Eve trailed after Adam, but there is no mention of it. God's anger was only at Adam.)

What did man do to cause God to expel him from paradise? It was not only that he disobeyed God. That was part of it; their behavior made them feel guilty in God's presence, and they hid from His sight when He came to the garden. But the text makes it clear that there was something special about the tree from which Adam and Eve ate, and that their expulsion had to do with the fruit of that particular tree. We know that the tree did not bear knowledge itself. Ignorance is not the bliss of Eden, for Adam could have knowledge of the garden, and he could know and name the creatures of the earth. Nor did the fruit of that tree confer on Adam and Even the ability to make distinctions — a kind of knowledge — for Adam could distinguish the animals and the fish and fowl God created. Nor was the tree's fruit their first taste of good or evil; remember, the primal two had every good thing in the garden, and Even knew the snake's venality but did not fall from her mere acquaintance with the evil serpent.

The meaning must be that they could distinguish good and evil as discrete concepts, separate from preference for and aversion to the things around them. "They fell from innocence when they knew and judged and did not act and enjoy" (Goodman, 1968a, pp. 143-4). The fall of Adam and Eve came when they learned to interrupt the free-functioning process of their living to make abstractions. So they covered their spontaneous sexuality with fig-leaf aprons, symbolizing the superimposition of the concept that nakedness is evil and shameful over their natural being.

Their sin was not only in disobeying God by eating of the tree of the knowledge of good and evil. Though their disobedience is a factor in what happened, our fall originates from more than feeling guilty because we have not been good children. The sin of Adam and Eve was in eating that particular fruit of the tree of the knowledge of good and evil. The fruit gave them the ability to know abstract concepts apart from their realization in the world and to live their lives (as they promptly began to do) deliberately, based on principles. So, by the fruit of that tree they became as we are, divorced from the union of awareness and expression, the synaptic experience of spontaneous and integrated behavior.

They ate only half the meal. To be godlike, the story says, they would also have had to have eaten of the tree of life. Those two together would have given them the knowledge of both the undifferentiated infinite, and of the willful differentiated particular — the id and ego modalities of the self — and they would have had eternal life, free of the turning of the six-spoked wheel. "We are sinful not merely because we have eaten of the Tree of Knowledge, but also because we have not yet eaten of the Tree of Life. The state in which we find ourselves is sinful quite independent of guilt" (Goodman, 1968a, p. 144 [He is quoting Kafka]).

Man's fall from grace, then, is in Gestalt terms the loss of our ability to give ourselves over to the synthetic process of gestalt formation. We traded our blithe accommodation to our environment for the ability to know things differently from their actuality and in this way to begin to impose ourselves on our environment. We live in the grip of our opinions and ideas, by plan and conception. We have left the fluid play of free functioning to the rest of creation; instead, we try to emulate notions we have constructed, and fit the universe to them as well. Our present is our clever fabrication. Our awareness is of our centrality and importance. But we are out of touch; we have no excitement. Having left our state of integration; we are suspended in the isolation of the distinctions we have made, and we do not taste life. We do not know how to care; we only know how to divide and reorganize.

While we are slaves to our mastery, the peacock spreads its fan. We are born, we live, we die. Everything is born, lives, dies, endures — and we say, half-full of the fruit of the tree of knowledge of good and evil, "Really, it is nothing but..."

In our understanding of this story, we should stress that our fall stems from the incompleteness of our picnic in Eden. Eating the fruit of the tree of knowledge of good and evil need not necessarily result in disaster. Many of our finest accomplishments are rooted in the abilities we gained when we partook of its fruit. Abstraction, cognition, intellection are keen tools, and the desire to try new ways of being — even if they break the rules — can come to beneficent invention. But to close the circle, we must add passion to the mind's razor edge and agility, and we must reinstate the sense of belonging to the community of nature we possessed before our fall. Therein is a new grace, the result of consciousness and spontaneity integrated.

The Origins of Disorder

> A neurotic is like Eliot's phrase: "You are nothing but a set of obsolete responses."
>
> *F. S. Perls*

This chapter is directed to what mental health professionals call neurosis, psychosis, abnormal behavior, and the seemingly limitless varieties of schizophrenia; it also covers their ordinary language versions: being crazy, being sick, being freaky, and being screwed, fucked, and hung up.

Few of these terms find much use in Gestalt therapy. The more casual ones recommend themselves by their lack of pretense, and the "clinical" ones are used occasionally in professional discourse, in the absence of anything better. But the more technical terms are deceptive, being less precise than they seem to be. Unlike much of the use of diagnostic categories in medicine, psychiatric labels do not suggest specific therapeutic actions. Labeling patients gives a false sense that we have accomplished something, that we have put our finger on the problem. All we have done is put our finger on our fingering.

The categories of "mental illness" have many clinical and social uses that, in fact, weigh against successful treatment. They imply we get schizophrenic as we get a cold, and they burden therapists, patients, and their families with stigmatic labels. Gestalt therapy does not use these categorizations because they are inimical to the Gestalt approach.

In the first place, disorders are not "mental," they are organismic. The mind-body split is itself a disordered mode of thinking. We are not sick in our minds; rather, *we* are sick — the whole of us is disturbed. What are called mental disorders are in the context of Gestalt therapy interferences with the process of gestalt formation and destruction, which result in distortions and imbalances in our basic integration. They are disorders of the functioning and growth of the self.

In the second place, these disorders of functioning are not fixed categories, as they so often seem to be in psychological terminology. Or rather, the categories are fixed, but our behavior is not. In Gestalt therapy, we understand that our characterizations of healthy and abnormal behavior are references to present processes. They represent our patient in this moment in time; as he changes, we think of him differently.

The characterization of disorder in Gestalt therapy is in terms of differences in the kind and quality of the discrepancy of the gestalt process of figure formation and destruction from its healthy, normal mode. We speak of disorders of contact or support, of difficulties in permitting the zero point to persist or appear, or the inability of the patient to let figures dissolve after they cease to be pertinent. We define abnormality in reference to the same processes we look to in defining health.

In an attempt to imply the stance toward "mental illness" stated here, we will use disorder, abnormality, dysfunction, interference, and disruption instead of the traditional terms. What is meant is disease — dis-ease, the lack of ease, the absence of free functioning.

Healthy functioning contains within it vulnerabilities. Our contact with the environment means we are constantly open to danger. Further, the process of gestalt formation insures that we become focused in our attention at some point. Oriented to the one event that interests us, we can be caught unawares, taken by surprise. We may find ourselves confronted by danger while our back is turned. Finally, adversity may persist and mount to the extent that we are, or feel we are, no longer able to deal with it. We are dependent on the environment, but it is not always able or willing to meet our needs. Deprivation of the resources we need to satisfy ourselves is a fact of our existence — though if we are fortunate it is an occasional liability and not a chronic one — and the field may be full of pitfalls.

Take the terrible despair of mourning. Living in a relationship that provides us great sustenance, we have turned the other into a Thou. By our engagement, we have made the other part of the gestalt of our experience, part of ourselves. And then the other is gone. The contact we have opened ourselves to is suddenly a contact with emptiness. We look into an abyss, and we become filled with grief and loss.

As children, the possibility of frustration, deprivation, and danger is greater than it is when we become adults, for the environment's rule in our growth is greater. We are less skilled at organizing the field so that the simple, basic needs we have are satisfied. In the ordering of things, our parents do for us some of the things we will do for ourselves later on. This is part of the relationship of parent and child. Development is a process of taking on the functions of independent manipulation of the field to meet our needs. But the possibility of misfortune looms large to us and is often realized in childhood, as the inadequacies of our parents interfere with their parenting.

Most disorders originate in childhood. A normal response of the healthy organism to prolonged difficulty has been referred to as our safety functions. These are emergency situations, and in an emergency we resort to the repertoire of protective behaviors — our safety functions — that are available to us. We blot out or distort contact at our boundaries, and we mobilize our behavior to operate at that level of functioning where we can best deal with what is happening. If mother will not feed us when we are hungry, we learn to ignore our hunger. Perhaps we resent her, but we also love her and need her, so we disregard our resentment or turn it elsewhere.

If the emergency persists, our emergency behavior persists. If we are filled with grief, and we are not permitted to rage against the circumstances or cry out our helplessness, we will make whatever adjustment we can. Perhaps we will cloak our grief with a masklike face — an emotionless death mask. We close the figure in the best possible way, given what the field — the environment, and our felt sense of emergency and threat — will tolerate.

In doing so, we must interfere with our own free functioning, suppressing the excitement that seeks to force us to the prohibited behaviors and the responses that are most appropriate for us, in favor of those that are acceptable. We turn against our spontaneous behavior out of what we perceive to be our needs in the situation. In doing so, we come into conflict with ourselves, and part of our life energy must go into restraining ourselves. Suppression, conscious and controlled, soon becomes unaware and chronic repression. We blot out the conflict in an attempt to obtain closure, and to free our attention for the newer exigencies of life — trials or pleasures — that are always awaiting us.

The problems with this kind of solution are these. First, we must persist in functioning as though there is an emergency, though it may pass. (As we get older, we can obtain our own food.) Second, we have disrupted our orienting and manipulating abilities; some of our possibilities are now lost to our awareness. (Remember, our safety functions are flight, withdrawal, desensitization, hallucination, delusion. They are distortions of contact that necessarily disrupt our ability to deal successfully with new situations.) Third, the energy that continues to go into the conflict of which we have become unaware is lost to us, so we cannot use it to deal with new situations. In disordered functioning, we are in a chronic crisis operating with our safety functions. Our facilities for normal, healthy, figure/ground formation and destruction are impaired, since we have repressed aspects of them. We must eliminate the possibility of crying, or rage, or laughter, for that might reinstate the claim of the gestalt we have not finished.

Some of our energies go into a stalemate of immobility. The conflict between our free functioning and what we feel we must do is not resolved by the solution we have made. Healthy unawareness comes from the destruction of the figure. Here, the process has been aborted prior to its conclusion. So, we must continue to restrain the momentum to closure that persists by the unfinished gestalt, or it will culminate in unacceptable behavior. We must also undercut the excitement that can go into other figures, for that too will excite our whole selves and reactivate the conflict within us.

Long after the event is past, we do not remember its details. Perhaps if we did, we would know that the field is different than it was then. Perhaps we are more capable, and our environment more tractable. If we retain any awareness, we usually know only that some undefined and grave fear is attached to certain behaviors. But that is enough, so our chronic impaired functioning persists, for the gravity of our fear is felt to be as large and fraught with our survival as it was when it occurred.

Disordered behavior is adjustments such as these. They are not healthy, for we do not function freely. There are creative adjustments in a field where some of the possibilities that might be available are not available. They are the best we can manage, given what appears to be possible.

What we call organismic disorder is the accumulation of events like these. By interference with our contact functions and the persistence of our safety functioning, we lost our unity. We are no longer in touch with ourselves, or with the environment, and our contact and excitement do not any more lead to a strong gestalt and expressive action.

As a result, we cannot grow. We are struck with the same behaviors we developed earlier. Old sensory and motor attitudes persist, though in new situations they must be inappropriate. Our energy is doubly defused — into the specific conflict between our free functioning and the impossible demands of the situation as we perceive them, and in the general restraint necessary to keep organismic excitation below the level where it would restimulate the conflict in spite of our repressing it.

The general intention of our safety functions is avoidance. Endangered, we can annihilate the other, or leave the scene. If these are not possible, we can withdraw our contact and repression, or construct a delusion or hallucination to intrude between us and the danger. Another possibility is to reorganize the field so we can be supported by it. One form this takes is regression — we become childish, dependent on the field to do for us what we feel we cannot do for ourselves. Taken together with the limits our safety functioning puts on us, we become sick and helpless, which is how we feel.

In abnormal functioning, the persistence of this set of behaviors means that we experience ourselves as lacking the means to deal with new situations, and since much of our potential is lost to us, this feeling is often accurate. Since our contact and support functions are impaired, we are likely to be inadequate. Consequently, many life situations are threatening to us, and we become generally phobic about living.

The typical ambiance of "neurosis" is the result. Our sense of our bodies is diminished, as is our sensory functioning. We cannot seem to be interested or excited, and much of what we do seems meaningless to us. We do not see what is in front of us, or can not avail ourselves of it. It is alien, and dull, just as we ourselves are. We feel empty, and confused. And even when we seem to know what we want to say or do, we have difficulty expressing ourselves.

Aspects of Abnormal Functioning — an Example

In terms of gestalt formation, abnormality is interrupting the gestalt at various aspects of its emergence. A simple way to talk about this is by using the simile of metabolism.

Our metabolic process — eating, digestion, and elimination — is a manifestation of the figure/ground phenomenon on the level of our physical being. As was pointed out in the first chapter, we are unified beings. Our processes have a dynamic similarity. Dealing with food is one aspect of our organismic functioning, and it works in basically the same way as our overall functioning. We have organismic appetites and processes — appetites for experiences, for emotional contact, for food. We deal with all of them in essentially the same way. Getting our teeth into a steak and getting our teeth into a life problem works out the same way; chewing over a theory and chewing over a bite of toast are dynamically similar. In both, we destroy old gestalts to create new ones. In eating, we destroy food, making our satisfaction and new tissue for our bodies.

We start early in life with a simple process, sucking on milk, swallowing it, transforming it into our selves. As we get older, we develop teeth. We become capable of biting off parts of the environment that need more concerted and forceful disintegrative measures to become part of our bodies. Our possibilities are enlarged, and we become able to eat solid foods with widely differing tastes and textures. By biting and chewing, we can gradually make them into small enough bits so our internal digestional system — peristalsis, the grinding action of our intestines, and the chemical solvent properties of our saliva and stomach juices — can complete their transformation of the food into the building materials of body tissue. In our terms, as we grow we become capable of creating and destroying more complex gestalts.

The first contact boundary here is our organs of taste and smell. They make the distinctions in coordination with our preferences. Another censor, further along in the process, is our disgust. If we take in things we don't need, our gagging reflex will be activated, and we will reject what we have begun to assimilate. This censoring process continues through the metabolic process. We may throw up food that becomes unacceptable at the point of the gastrointestinal tract. Finally, we will expel as waste that part of what we have taken in that we cannot use for energy or body tissue.

We can see that eating is an instance of the general case of figure formation. For example, our balance is disturbed by a deficit in protein and a desire to taste sweetness. Differentiating the field, we become aware of the parameters of appetite, and out of what is in the pantry, we find something that seems to meet our needs. This is the emergent figure — milk and cookies, for example. Obtaining what we need, we chew and swallow it, and we digest it. Part of what we have taken in is retained as metabolic energy and body cells, while the rest is eliminated. We have destroyed our hunger; it is no longer figure. We are sated.

Interference with this total process can occur at any point in it. Initially, the first differentiations of the gestalt, we may lose touch with what we need, or with what is available for our consumption. As a result, we take in things we don't need, or we don't seek out what we do need. Further, we cannot get the satisfaction that comes with our awareness of manipulating ourselves and the environment to get what we need.

Later, with the gestalt fully formed, we can fail to use our incisors and molars well, swallowing large pieces of food and obliging our digestive tract to produce large quantities of stomach acids to dissolve the chunks of food; or we may choose a steady diet of soft foods that do not need hearty chewing. Either course robs us of satisfaction.

What we can see in this example are the possibilities of distortion in the process of figure/ground formation. Disruptions in our awareness of the nature of our appetite or of what will satisfy us are disorders of contact in the early differentiation phase of gestalt formation. Here we find problems like not knowing if we are hungry or not, confusing hunger with other feelings — anxiety, for example — and not knowing what we wish to eat. Disruptions in biting, chewing, and swallowing are similes for dysfunctions in contact, differentiation, and figure destruction. Familiar problems here include tearing off bits of food instead of biting them, chewing food particles insufficiently to permit their easy assimilation into our metabolic processes, and gulping down chunks of food whole. Diarrhea, constipation, and indigestion are difficulties in figure destruction that stem from earlier failures of adequate functioning. Their counterparts in the area of vocal expression, for example, are excessive thoughtless speech (running on at the mouth, often called verbal diarrhea), inadequacies in articulation, and confused speech, respectively.

Interferences in the Modes of the Self

We have seen earlier that the self functions in two basic dimensions, engagement and style. The interferences described above are all impediments to our engagement, or contact, in the present situation. This is characteristic of impaired functioning. In organismic disorders, however, both the style and engagement dimensions of the self are impaired. In fact, the disruption of the modes of the self is essential to our being able to interfere with free functioning. The means by which we conceive of and execute the strategy we impose onto our organismic behavior is the self in the mode of ego.

In the malfunctioning of the modalities of the self, the interplay between ego and id modes is disrupted. Typically, it is the mode of ego that assumes an unhealthy dominance. And it is easy to see why. Malfunctioning comes out of dangerous situations. Endangered, we experience ourselves as potentially injured by the process we are involved in. Initially, our response is the middle mode that we have termed our safety functions. But when the felt danger persists and at the same time we must deal with other, newer exigencies, we act to obliterate our safety function reactions. This act is the first imbalance, the prime assertion of our isolated willfulness over our integrated behavior. It is in ego mode activity that we experience ourselves as making the situation turn out as we want, so it is that mode which comes to the fore in the kind of continual danger we have described. When things seem to be getting out of hand, we can be in control.

In this situation, the persistence of our ego functioning halts the flux of the self, for we feel the normal give and take of the organism/environment field isn't enough to ensure an outcome that will meet our needs. Id and ego are no longer the cooperative, integrated styles of the self. Instead, the mode of ego is imposed on the self's functioning. We shoulder out the balanced middle mode behavior which combines the id and ego modes.

Simultaneously, our boundaries, which become clear and well defined in ego functioning, maintain that distinctness. We encircle ourselves in protection against the hostile outside, like wagons in an Indian attack. What is outside our boundaries is oppressive, and hostile. Contact and withdrawal do not move smoothly into one another any more. Now, we "make" contact, and hold on; or withdraw into isolation. We have made a thing out of the process of our living. Flow is stilled, replaced by stilted changes; boundaries are firm, contact is severely diminished, excitement is shunned, and we treat ourselves as objects of threat to be manipulated and mastered. We have reified ourselves.

The rigidification of the self's boundary in the ego mode is further enhanced by the diminished awareness of the self in danger. Seeing with blinders, deliberation cannot do the trick, for the data we have to work with are too scanty to fit the facts. Though we continue to exist in an unique situation, our plans are generalities. Our programming does not help. With each failure, we are confirmed in the belief of our danger, for we still are not gratified.

In health, we aim for completion. Impaired, we aim for victory, and stave off defeat. Feeling ourselves endangered, we have adopted with seeming finality a mode of functioning that we believe best ensures our existence; it is experienced as identical with our control over a situation that threatens to get out of hand. Our satisfaction and sense of self comes, then, in conquest and control. We strive to dominate, or to eliminate what we cannot control. When we have mastered the field, we might feel secure.

Since much of what we need to control is ourself, we can understand these disorders as self-conquests. We act to eliminate the danger by eliminating the excitement and awareness that might again endanger us. Much of that comes from us, so we must be vigilant in avoiding anything that might reactivate free functioning, since our danger would surely be its first figure. We come to be like two prizefighters in a perpetual clinch.

The same need for control means we attempt to manipulate the other aspects of the field — the objects and people of our environment. We must do all we can to make things turn out right for us. Yet our involvement and excitement are reduced. So, we urge, persuade, cajole, lie, in order to have people do what we would, in health, do for ourselves. At the same time that we are trying to be masterful, we are being dependent. The purpose of our control is to perpetuate an infant's state, where the environment meets most of our needs without our having to take part in the dialectic and excitement of the gestalt process. Of course, we are not infants, but our manipulations are how we restrict our involvement and infantilize ourselves.

An alternate response to danger, primary in certain "psychoses" but common to most disorders is the self-functioning persistently in the mode of the id. Id functioning offers our threatened self a retreat. If we think of continued, impaired, ego functioning as the solidification of the self into willfulness for the purpose of exercising maximum control, we can think of continued impaired id functioning as the dissolution of the self into the background for the purpose of avoiding danger. We become like a field bird frozen at the crack of a twig — it tries to disappear, its feathers a camouflage.

Remember, the quality of id functioning is that it is loose, energetic, and associative, close to the flux of the undifferentiated field. In id functioning we experience the energy of contact but we do not experience much of the separateness of ourselves. We are part of the field. Our boundaries are only vaguely felt, our activities seem almost not to emanate from us. In frozen id functioning, we lose the context of swinging from id to ego modes according to circumstances. Our nonexistence becomes the pervasive character of our functioning. Even what we do seems to happen to us, our actions do not take subject or object. We become out of touch and impulse ridden. Seemingly spontaneous, we are only our excitement and fear spilling out.

A seeming paradox of persisting id functioning is that its very persistence is a function of the ego's mode. The fixity of id functioning means that we have acted to maintain it. That act of maintenance is an ego mode act.

We can also see the reverse. While the ego is deliberate, in disordered functioning its focus is often fixed on different figures quite quickly, attempting to prevent any of them from evolving into excitement. Nevertheless, all disorders are (first) disruptions of the self in which the ego predominates inappropriately, for disruption is an instance of making things happen, and is therefore a capability of the ego mode.

It is important to stress that neither disordered id functioning nor disordered ego functioning exists by itself. But each persists inappropriately and out of balance with its polar opposite. The gestalts we form are held and maintained by us. In the mode of ego, we lose track of much of the background; in id, we seldom get beyond it. The persistence of these modalities — healthy at the right moment — are impaired behavior. The rhythmic alternation of id and ego, a quality of the normal self that comes of full and present contact with the changing situation, is absent. The impaired organism does not have good contact, and so it cannot be spontaneous or balanced. It can only be rigid, or preyed on by its impulses.

It is not simply that the id and ego modes of the self persist beyond their appropriateness in abnormal functioning. In health, ego and id are two sides of a coin — they work in concert, and the self *is* these two modalities. One may predominate at some times, but in their healthy activity, they are always in interaction. As part of integrated functioning, they can be distinguished but not separated, any more than we can talk about one side of a seesaw without considering the other, or a husband without considering a wife. They are the connected aspects of a single gestalt, an interactive system. In disordered functioning, they are dislodged both from the ground of their interaction with each other and from full contact with the gestat, since our awareness is diminished. Consequently, like an engine racing, out of gear, or running on an oil slick road, they take on a disproportionate aspect. Each loses the play, flexibility, refinement, and restraint that come of their constant interplay with reality and each other.

Take the example of a couple. The wife is responsive, energetic, forceful. The husband is conscientious, disciplined, direct, low-keyed. In a good relationship, they complement each other. When things are not good, the wife's attractive vivaciousness becomes hysteria. She runs around, doing a million things, easily hurt and unsatisfied. She becomes nagging and demanding. The husband, on the other hand, becomes withdrawn, so quiet, even-tempered, and concerned with his responsibilities that he is depressed and dull. He loses the occasional moments of lightness he and his wife enjoyed so much. Their alternative ways of being complemented each other when they were in good contact with each other and had a viable relationship. Now, there is unfinished business between them. Both are dissatisfied, and withdraw from each other. As a consequence, their individual styles become isolated and ingrown. Lacking the counterbalance of the other's, her exuberance becomes hysteria, his solidness becomes sluggishness. Healthy ego and id functioning become impaired in the same way, from lack of contact and awareness, and in this same way does the impairment exaggerate and change the qualities of each of the modes. Energy without form becomes undefined, meaningless activity — impulses run rampant. Structure without excitement is going through the motions, deadness.

Interferences with Contact

Awareness, as we have seen, is being in the present. Abnormal functioning undercuts the now, deflecting our involvement to the middle zone of conscious mental process. The outer zone is the environment, the inner zone is us. The middle zone is our thoughts, fantasies, wishes. In abnormality, the middle zone is concerned with reducing our engagement. We do this by attending inappropriately and inordinately to the past and the future, to judgments and to opinions.

We may have anticipatory fantasies of great success and satisfaction, or ones of catastrophe. Planning, we miss the present. We may keep in mind our past experience comparing and judging the present in terms of the past, responding to our expectations rather than the current situation. Nothing is new — everything becomes a modification of a previous event, or a shadow of our preconceptions.

Perhaps we are fond of generalizations about the field. Then our experiences are instances of rules of human behavior — "I did that because I was irritated." The doing and irritation take a back seat to the explanation, to our fitting our experience into a framework. Or we are always wondering why events occur. We look past what is happening in front of us, not seeing the present, out of touch with it. Looking for explanations, we fail to apprehend what is happening.

Finally, we may live in our memories, relishing our recollections. The result, though, is the same. We do not see that we have made an error — the present moment is different from the past. This is taking thought as an interposition against free functioning, reliving the fall of Adam and Eve.

There is in Gestalt therapy a healthy respect for the power and importance of thought and language. The development of higher cognition in man has made possible the discovery and development of rationality, in the forms of logic and measurement, and promotedmany extensions of man's creative potential. The development of sophisticated language skills along with these advanced intellectual processes has allowed us to evolve styles of speech and writing capable of precision and poetic evocation. Well used, language permits us to convey experience, to speak beyond what we have experienced, and to make new experiences in the processes of writing and communication. Truly it is a remarkable tool.

But, like all our capabilities, speech and thought can be realized in ways that reduce our ability to function adequately and satisfy ourselves. They can be used to defuse us. They can come between our contact with the world, so we don't really see or hear; they can replace our active encounter with what is outside us in favor of autistic mutterings. These activities, inappropriate and ineffective protective measures, are expressions of ourselves in disunity. They are mentation cut off from the healthy excitement that is rooted in our physical existence and contact. It is wheel spinning, going nowhere.

(Gestalt's lingo here is "mind fucking." To mind fuck is to mentate or speak out of touch with our excitement and our needs. It replaces the old-fashioned but equally pungent "bullshit." Unfortunately, "mind fucking" is often used imprecisely, as an expletive of derision when the other is thinking, without regard for the aptness of the thoughts or the activity of thinking. All intellection is not mind fucking, only intellection that is an evasion.)

Here is Don Juan:

"You talk to yourself too much, you're not unique at that. Every one of us does that. We carry on internal talk. Think about it. Whenever you are alone, what do you do?"

"I talk to myself."

"What do you talk about?"

"I don't know, anything, I suppose."

"I'll tell you what we talk to ourselves about. We talk to ourselves about our world. In fact, we maintain our world with our internal talk..."

"How can I stop talking to myself?"

"First of all you must use your ears...A warrior is aware that the world will change as soon as he stops talking to himself and he must be prepared for that monumental jolt."

(In Casteneda, A Separate Reality, *Simon & Schuster, 1971, p. 263)*

As our experience of our mentation replaces our experience of the unified field, the cohesive organismic intelligence that is intuition is replaced by its cognitive component, the intellect. We soon fail to grasp the unity of ourselves and the various others of the field — objects and people, friends, lovers, enemies — that grows out of our involvement with them and the excitement of our interaction. Our relationships no longer have the organic form that comes from that kind of contact. Instead, we organize our relationships according to abstract principles like fairness, rights or freedom, and we put our principles in a privileged position ahead of the demands of any particular situation. Organic form, the organization that comes out of a situation, is replaced by mechanical form. Concepts of fairness, right, good, justice — the gamut of ethical and moral considerations — spring up to fill the void we have created by the vacuity of our experience and the autistic quality of our contact. Says the Tao:

> When the great way falls into disuse
> There are benevolence, and rectitude

Language is predisposed to our use of it to interfere with contact and experience. It is, we have seen, structurally organized to permit us to estrange ourselves from others, from our feelings, and from our acts. We can speak without being involved, without responsibility. "It is said," we say, though the referent is not "it," but our own pain. "It can't be helped," we reply to another's distress, instead of saying directly, "I can't help you," or more accurately, "I will not help you," or "I do not want to help you." We blunt the interaction and blur the distinctions, seemingly to protect others, but in fact to protect ourselves.

The quality of our speech reflects our unhealthy use of it. It becomes thick, dull, inaccessible, as it is used to fill our voids. The poetry of color and surprise that is the verbal counterpart of lively functioning becomes interminable and prosaic.

Talking serves many of the same avoidance purposes in disordered functioning that thinking does. Instead of coordinating with the rest of our experience and enhancing our contact, it replaces both. We speculate, surmise, talking about events rather than from them. Or we drive our experiences away from us. Speaking about them, we dissipate their excitement and push them away from us with our chatter. Our experiences do not have a chance to settle into us and make their impression; we wriggle out of their grasp by speaking.

> When a fish meets the fish hook
> If he is too greedy he will be caught
> When his mouth opens
> His life is already lost.

Our attempts to disrupt our own free functioning take two general forms, interference or substitution, and repression. They usually occur together, in tandem, or in temporal proximity. We talk, for example, to distract ourselves from our concerns and also to exhaust the energy they generate. As part of our self-conquest, we must fight the motoric activity that would express our concerns, grinding ourself to a halt; then, we eliminate that conflict from our awareness, in part by forcing our attention elsewhere.

The repressive aspects of our obstruction of ourselves stem in part from the persistence of aspects of our normal functioning. Repression is the forgetting of suppressed activity. Suppressing our motor responses is part of our repertoire of responses to danger. It can be seen in many other animals: standing stock-still, alert, breath held. In health, it is usually a momentary response, dissolving into action when the possibilities of the field have been assessed. Excitement coursing through the organism is braked for a moment, until the situation directs it into the appropriate channels. Suppressing our spontaneous responses is retroflection. As we pointed out in the last chapter, its healthy aspect is self-control, self-restraint in the service of gaining skills and mastery. For example, we learn to tighten our sphincter against the impulse to defecate until we can be at a toilet.

Our forgetting is also rooted in normal behavior. It is our facility for ignoring, becoming unaware of those parts of the field that either hold no interest for us or that we have finished with. At the early stages of gestalt formation, this involves contacting loosely all the elements of the field in order to assess their relevance, and then leaving behind what we can not use. Our contact is neutral; often, we don't even retain the impression they made on us. At the end of the gestalt process, forgetting is part of destroying the now irrelevant figure.

In repression, our deliberate inhibition of our impulses is forgotten. The danger of acting is still present, but there is nothing further to be done about the problem. Our awareness fades. We no longer know how we are in conflict with ourselves, but all the same our excitement is bound up. An urge to fight, to cry, to shit, to make love was halted by a contrary reaction against that urge. In the press of new business, or our growing disinterest in the face of the chronicity of the impasse, we forget. (Remember, it is normal to become desensitized to sameness; our sensory bias is to novelty.)

As we lose touch with our conflicts, the functioning of our self becomes limited. We have given up aspects of our impulses, feelings and actions. Over our basic physiology, unified with the total organism, we impose a secondary physiology of emergency restraints, which then become chronic and habitual. They become the us we know, a second nature of learned responses to crisis. Chronically contracted, tensed against ourself and the no longer dangerous environment, our musculature is like a protective shell. It becomes what Reich called an armor, a shield against our organismic strivings and the encroachments of the environment.

Repression is a misleading term for this process. In holding ourselves back, we do not simply stop our functioning. The excitement we have mustered does not disappear. Energy cannot be created or destroyed, and the energy of our existence, impeded from moving into the coming gestalt, must go somewhere. Our excitement is not stopped. It is blocked, and is transformed into the process of blocking, and perhaps also into other substitute activities. We transform the accumulation of excitement from the free-functioning process to another. We may be able to find acceptable components in the field from which to make a gestalt that will satisfy us. If the momentum of our original figure/ground can find other components of similar importance to us, we may be able to direct our excitement into the new figure with great enthusiasm.

However, substitute figures are usually inadequate to meet the needs that occasioned the original figure. To some extent, they will not satisfy, and this inadequacy increases as the substitutes fall farther away from our desire. So, we force ourself to attend to something we do not care about. We listen politely to dull conversation. Inevitably, then, we are obliged both to hold part of ourself back and to push part of ourself ahead. We are always driving with the brake and accelerator depressed. We move forward and expend ourself, but we lack incentive, grace, and daring.

While this process serves to stop the original expression of our needs, the resultant armor has its own distinctive qualities. We repress the expression of our needs, but not the needs themselves. In holding ourselves back, we express the holding back of our needs. In a distorted and oblique fashion, we also therefore express the need.

Repressing rage may be expressed by drawing our lips tightly together, keeping our mouth shut and covering our biting teeth. Our face may become gray and colorless from denying it the energy it would use to come to our moment of anger. So, we draw our blood away from our surface. Or our general capacity to express ourselves deeply may be repressed; the depth and mobility of our face may be replaced with a flawless, glassine-perfect complexion, denying ourselves the possibility of knowing our responses.

Since our control is bound to be imperfect, it sometimes happens that we began to relax our inhibitions. We may begin to find our level of excitement matching or exceeding the force of our inhibitions, for our needs are still trying to move to fulfillment, the figure wants to emerge. The resulting battle of excitement and constriction is what is called anxiety.

Anxiety is the conflict of our attempts to block our excitement. It happens when we interrupt the emerging gestalt. Physiologically, anxiety is our contraction of our chest against our organismic need to supply the oxygen necessary to support the new excitement. When we doubt that we can follow through with the mounting flood of energy we feel, we try to suppress it. "Anxiety as an emotion is the dread of one's own daring" (Perls, Hefferline, and Goodman, 1951, p. 413). Anxiety is originally our experience of the conflict between our organismic needs and the constraints of our safety functions; later, when we have institutionalized our safety functions, it is the conflict of our armor and our excitement. At this later stage, we are likely to recognize neither for what they are; our experience is only of our discomfort.

Anxiety is a repression that is incomplete. We have not succeeded in conquering ourselves. We are not yet rendered immobile; our armor has chinks. In anxiety, we are in touch with the present mounting excitement, and we are also in touch with our expectations of the outcome of expressing our excitement. The conflict is between the present forming figure and our anticipation of disaster should we continue to allow the figure to develop. Only partly involved in the present happening, we allow our fantasies of the future to serve the purpose of undercutting our excitement. This is the dynamic of which stage fright is an example. Looking to the coming performance, our energy surges; but it isn't time for the show. We have no outlet for our excitement, so we restrain it as we wait. The result is what we experience as anxiety.

Taken all together, these behaviors constitute what are called our defenses. They arise out of our attempts to protect ourself and maintain our functioning, but they become and are better understood as aggressions against the self. Our defenses are as defensive as the United States Department of Defense, and the enemy is within.

Unfinished Business

If we are out of touch with many of our possibilities, we cannot satisfy ourselves. In these circumstances, the gestalts we make cannot fully reflect our needs, and their resolution similarly is unfulfilling. We accumulate unfinished business.

Unfinished business is organismic indigestion. We become clogged with foreign matter, the uncompleted gestalts that are the result of our interference with free functioning.

> Tanzan and Ekido were once travelling together down a muddy road. A heavy rain was still falling.
> Coming around a bend they met a lovely girl in a silk kimono and sash, unable to cross the intersection.
> "Come on, girl," said Tanzan at once. Lifting her in his arms, he carried her over the mud.
> Ekido did not speak again until that night when they reached a lodging temple. Then he could no longer restrain himself. "We monks don't go near females," he told Tanzan, "especially young and lovely ones. It is dangerous. Why did you do that?"
> "I left the girl there," said Tanzan. "Are you still carrying her?"

We begin by carrying around our repressions — the armory of our self-conquest. With our awareness blocked and our energies diminished, we cannot bring enough of ourselves to new situations. Lacking our full participation, the new gestalts are weak, and incomplete. We leave ourselves hanging. We accumulate incomplete, hung-up emotions like resentment and worry, to match our incomplete behavior. Over time, we collect a queue of incomplete situations, unspoken sentences, recurrent dreams, unexpressed urges. "As a rule of thumb, it is never what you *do* that makes you neurotic, but what you don't do" (Glasgow, 1971, p. 96).

As every gestalt strives to closure, every bit of unfinished business we have strives to be finished. Everything we have repressed wants to get out. Our urges cannot be forgotten or repressed; only their expression can. On the physical level, unfinished business is the stalemate of motoric impulses and our armored musculature. Sometimes we feel it as chronic aches, or surprising sensitivity or insensitivity in areas of our body.

Our unfinished business is the animator of the compulsions and obsessions so frequent in abnormal functioning. They are our attempts to bring past incomplete gestalts to closure. They continue to be unsuccessful because they remobilize our resistance to them. Most of our seemingly irrational acts, acting out, can be understood in the same way. They come from the hidden agenda of the self trying to establish organismic self-regulation at a more thorough and satisfactory level.

These actions are commonly referred to as symptoms. Symptoms are both expressions of our organismic vitality, and at the same time, attacks on our vitality by ourselves. They are expressions of our conflicts. We are both prisoner and jailer, master and slave. The gestalt is hidden, but it is so strong that it shows itself in the shape of the symptomatic behavior of our impaired functioning. In Gestalt therapy, symptoms are understood to be attempts to solve an important problem for us in the best way we can, given our limited awareness of our situation.

The Individual and Society

This discussion has emphasized the role of the individual in constructing his own misfortune. We are the architects of our misery. At the same time, we have seen that we originally learn to master ourselves largely in response to interpersonal demands, for there was a time when our continued existence depended on acquiescing to the demands of the environment.

As adults, we are more capable now than we were of making our own situations to suit us. But we are still imbedded in the field, and our circumstances are often less inclined to our satisfaction than they could be. Social structures — the political system, our work or schooling, our social and familial relations — are made up of the desires of our fellowmen and ourselves. All of us to some extent share the impairment of "normality," and as a consequence our personal needs and the demands of the environment often do not coincide.

In many ways we can understand the conflicts within us that have been described above as conflicts between our organismic and social existences. The imperatives of the social scene are often not so different from what they were when we were infants. The social scene is replete with rules, norms, and laws to govern our behavior. There is a correct way to live, and it is enforced by the subtle or blunt pressures of society. We should be such and such. Every culture has these shoulds. As standards of behavior, they must limit our free functioning. A certain amount of this is a small price for the satisfactions that an adequate social order can provide. But in a culture as unhealthy as this one often is, social demands disallow major aspects of our natures.

Difficult as it is, the picture is not hopeless. One of the positive aspects of this society is its diversity, mobility, and lack of cohesion. There have always been some places where we can go to find surroundings that allow us more adequate choices. These days their number is increasing along with the general relaxation of social inhibitions. It is often possible to carve out a private niche wherein we can try to do what best satisfies us. But because of our legacy of unfinished business and impaired functioning, we often cannot avail ourselves of these opportunities. (Nor are they much use if we feel strongly about broader social issues like the destruction of Asian civilization or the exploitation of our natural and social resources.)

The issue here is: to what extent is our health dependent on our surroundings and to what extent is it dependent on us? On the one hand it should be clear that from the standpoint of Gestalt therapy the single criteria for health is our continuing ability to create and destroy gestalts. If we can embrace all of the field and allow its elements to dance to a single rhythm, we are healthy. On the other hand, if the field is impoverished, our figures will certainly lack richness, and our ability to make figures at all may be hampered. One of the qualities of the figures we make in such circumstances will be their impoverishment and inadequacy. If there isn't enough to eat to satisfy our needs for protein, vitamins, and minerals, we will be undernourished.

From one point of view, our impoverishment and our death are not unhealthy. If we proceed with full awareness of our existence, the environment and the ebb and flow of gestalt functioning, whatever occurs is simply the best way the field can be organized, given the possibilities. From another point of view, persistent danger and inadequacy in the field cannot help but render the prospects for creating figures and coming to closure more difficult. It is possible to live in a concentration camp and be healthy — we know that from the last world war. But that achievement requires such a heroic effort that many of us may not be able to muster it. And we need not look that far away to find these difficult situations. The experience of many of us growing up and living in civilization raises the same question.

We can resolve this issue if we acknowledge that an adequate answer does not require us to take one side or the other. For we can see the merits of both points of view: yes, our health depends on us, and yes, it also depends on what the field will permit. Perhaps this analogy will be clarifying. We are flowers. Within each of us is the seed of our potential. As we grow, we grow in accord with our possibilities. (In our case, the different possibilities of being human.) In the conditions are good, if there is adequate sunlight, warmth, and nourishment, we will bloom with the beauty of which we are capable. To the extent that the climate doesn't provide us with all of what we need for our full flowering, we will bloom differently — in other, perhaps less radiant hues, in varying sizes and strengths, turned or even twisted one way or the other, for a day or a week or a month. But no matter what, we will be some kind of flower, for we must grow according to our potential. So the shape of our existence is determined by our natures and by the possibilities of our environment.

As it stands, though, our analogy is not an adequate parallel to our actual situation. First, we are not only flowers, we are also our own gardeners. While we cannot command the sun and the rain, we can manipulate our environment to some degree. We can change our position to take the best advantage of the sun. Sometimes we can provide ourselves with water, nutrients, shelter. We are not victims of our circumstances, we have some measure of control over the components of our healthy growth.

Secondly, and decisively, we always have the alternative of maintaining our consciousness of our life as we live it. Even in the most dire of circumstances, this is open to us, and from the perspective of Gestalt therapy, we are healthy so long as we realize this possibility. From this perspective, satisfaction comes not from being happy or well fed but from being in touch with all of our life as we live it. If the fruits of the field are small, dried out, and insufficient, our experience will be of what we lack. And that is our existence. Our satisfaction, the fulfillment of our humanity, is in knowing our existence — our sadness and regret, if we come to that — knowing our existence in such a way that it pervades all of us, so there is no difference possible between what we know and what we are, what we are aware of and what we do. Our fulfillment comes not in being happy or unhappy, but in being.

Strategies of Abnormal Functioning

Abnormal functioning, pathological gestalt formation, is how we refer to the same configurations of behavior that are called complexes, neurosis, psychosis, schizophrenia. One difference between these two sets of terms is that the Gestalt terms emphasize process, and the other terms emphasize stasis. In organizing and conceptualizing behavior as we are doing here, it is difficult not to convey the sense that we are talking about concrete things. As we talk about regularities, their reoccurrence gives them a continuing presence, as though they occupy time and space: the persistence of repressing is repression.

Abnormality lends itself more easily to reification than does health, for abnormality is itself a reification. It consists of imposing ourselves on the gestalt process by holding on to certain intentions and modes of behavior. The uniqueness of normal health is replaced by the recurrent strategies of impairment.

There are some typical and notable strategies in abnormal functioning. They are the recurrent forms that our interference with our basic health takes. In tune with our emphasis on process, these forms are styles of impaired contacting and impaired coordination of the styles of the self, rather than diagnostic categories. In Gestalt therapy, we understand that all deviations from health are digressions of the engagement and style of the self. On the one hand, contact with the field is reduced, and we are instead in touch with the delusions and fantasies we have made. We live in our middle zone. On the other hand, ego and id functioning no longer are coordinated aspects of the self. They lose their balance and proportion and become grotesque. We become rigid and stuck, or diffuse, never quite apt.

What is lively and hopeful about impaired functioning is that the domination of our free functioning by our intentions is never complete. It must always be maintained by us. Impaired and distorted, we are a constant battleground between id and ego, between delusion and reality, between fear and need. Our urge to healthy functioning cannot be extinguished; the battle is never won. We always have the possibility of contacting and realizing the self anew.

Manifestations of impaired functioning originate in our dissatisfaction with the gestalt process. We and the demands of the environment come to be out of accord. We become endangered by the demands of the field, and we experience ourselves as unable to work out the difficult circumstances. Perhaps, when we were infants, this was true; now, we made it true by submitting to our own conquest.

Resultantly, we try to make ourselves over to meet the situational demands. We falsify ourselves because we do not accept what we are. After all, what we are is not good enough. This dissatisfaction is our invitation to use our ego mode functioning to redo ourself. Desiring to be other than we are means that our felt boundaries are no longer coincident with our actual boundaries. We block out what ever does not correspond to the ideal image we have constructed, our self-concept. We hope we can make it with this new person we have made up. We come to have both a self and a self-concept, and we attempt to force ourself into the image we have conceived.

We will, of course, try to fit the rest of the field into the same procrustean bed. The environment also has to fit our idealization if we are to succeed. These two are aspects of the same dissatisfaction. Out of it, we change ourselves and what is outside us. As we embrace our conception of our basic inadequacy, the door to impairment opens.

Each of the characteristic ways the self contacts the rest of the field has a counterpart in abnormal functioning. Healthy confluence, projection, introjection, and retroflection have pathological outcomes as our contact with the field and the modalities of the self are disturbed. Confluence becomes pseudoconfluence, fantasied alterations in the environment become projection, role playing and imitation become introjection, and self-control becomes retroflection.

As confluence is the appreciation of sameness, pseudoconfluence is making the individual and the environment the same. Here, we pathologically keep the field undifferentiated, giving up our knowledge of the difference of ourselves and the environment. Infantlike, we hold to the original confluence of breast and child. Our mouths are always open. We do not assimilate experience, we just gulp it in. We experience no boundaries, no sense of ourselves as distinct from what is outside us. We cannot make contact, for contact is the appreciation of the differences we have become unable to know. We cannot form a figure. We cling to our lack of awareness; like children, we are unable to play our own part in changing our circumstances, for we feel we lack the ability to do anything. The other must make all the effort, for we are helpless. We are as though in a trance, without will, without any functioning of the ego mode at all.

Eric Hoffer's true believer and the members of Charles Manson's family are well-known recent examples of pseudoconfluent functioning. The true believer is a person who seeks out a movement or cause to involve himself in. The precise nature of the cause is secondary to the true believer's need to secure his identification with it, so that he can lose his individuality in it. He can be a rabid communist and later on a rabid fascist. What is necessary for him is to be so intensely committed to his beliefs that they fill the vacuum of his empty self. Then all his decisions are made and all his behavior ordered in response to the dictates of the system in which he has absorbed himself. Pseudoconfluence is escaping from ourself.

What is called "laying a trip" — being told how we ought to feel or act and accepting it for whatever reason — is effective only because of our predilection for pseudoconfluence. Trips are laid on those who will take them; we get trips laid on us in accordance with our willingness to give up our gestalt digestive process and gulp in another's view of ourself. (Note that this is an interaction. We must acquiesce in this transaction: We get the security of being infants, the other the security of controlling us.)

Projection stems from our ability to isolate those aspects of the environment that are important to us, as part of the forming of a figure to meet our needs. A preliminary aspect of this is testing our conception of what changes we need to make in the field by fantasying alterations in it. In healthy functioning, we retain the knowledge that our fantasies are our doing, and that what exists is not the same as what we are conceiving. In pathological projection, the boundary of distinction between what is us and what is not us is lost. We see the world as we want it to be, and then we lose track of what we have done to the outside world; we come to believe that the way we have made things is in fact how it is. So, we ignore our wife's kindness and project onto her our mother's coldness.

There are two parts to projection, whether it be healthy or impaired. First, we wipe out reality, obliterating the actual. Next, we fill the blank we have made with our fantasy. In abnormal functioning, we cease to be aware of what we have done. Unhealthy projection requires that we avoid any responsibility for distorting reality. So, we alienate our feeling of coldness, and attribute it to our wife. We give away our feelings. Being unaware of this, we do not notice that important aspects of ourselves are no longer parts of us, and that the world we see is a figment of our fear. "We sit in a house lined with mirrors and think that we are looking out" (F. S. Perls, 1947, p. 158).

The necessity for projection is in our feeling that we cannot survive and possess our ideas and feelings, for they threaten to involve us in situations that we believe endanger us. So we disown them. Using the mechanism of projective contact, we put our anger, our demands, our abilities into others. Instead of experiencing our own needs or our disappointments, we feel ourselves demanded of, or perceive dissatisfaction all around us. Instead of knowing our own power, we feel ourselves helpless to resist the forceful insistence of others. We impoverish ourselves. We no longer experience what we have disowned. We split ourselves apart from them, setting up a boundary between what we can accept of ourselves and what we cannot. We are no longer whole. Where we had aspects we cannot endure, we come to have voids, for we have emptied parts of ourself onto the environment. We become childishly helpless, for we cannot experience parts of ourselves, and to that extent we cannot be in our own custody. We remain immature, dependent.

In introjection, as in confluence, we gulp down what is outside our boundaries without digesting them. But where confluence is a behavior of the breast-feeding infant — an id mode strategy, where our sense of a distinct self is almost nonexistent — introjection is a more discriminatory function. It is a more mature, precise attempt to deal with our felt inadequacy. It is an ego mode strategy. We try to remedy our inadequacies, filling the voids within us by taking on discrete attitudes and behaviors that we feel will help us survive. Introjecting, we first take on bits and pieces of roles we hope will allow us to deal successfully with situations that our spontaneous responses seem not to resolve; then, we lose our awareness of being actors. We forget that we have put on a mask, and soon we forget we are underneath. We think we are our roles.

Here, as in pseudoconfluence, the taking in is a pseudometabolism. What we take in and become is not assimilated into the self. The gestalt dialectic is bypassed, so the new ways we become cannot mesh with our essential self. Instead of being integrated and unified, we have layers.

We introject the origins of our distress. Usually, they are people who seem to force us to be as they wish. Originally, our parents are usually the inspiration for our introjects. Later, as we become dependent on this way of getting through the world, they come from others as well. They may be people we love, or people we don't love. If it is the former, our willingness to give up our gestalt process is greater, for we are linked to them by our desire to continue to have their affection. What is essential in order for us to introject is that they are, or are seen to be, in control of the situation, and therefore of us. They dominate us. They win, we lose. So we become like Quislings, identifying with the enemy. We cannot win, so we join them, taking on the power they have or we attribute to them. We go over to the other side, the party in power, the winning valence.

Like all recourses of our disordered functioning, this maneuver of ours does not satisfy us. We have bypassed our own needs and the process of the self working out their realization. We need to eat the specific food that our organismic self-regulation requires, and we need to bite it, chew it, digest it, and absorb it. Introjecting, we do none of these. We gulp down the big and little bits of behavior as we are becoming Helen Deutsch's "as-if personality." We are always playing a part, and none of the parts we play have verisimilitude or power, for they are out of touch with our energy. Our introjects do not suffice because we have not learned to cope, but only to copy. The changes of the environment face us with new circumstances, and all we can meet them with is a stale repertoire of old moves salvaged from unfinished situations and unresolved conflicts.

Also an aspect of impaired ego mode functioning is retroflection, the pathologic manifestation of self-control. Retroflection is our solution to our unwillingness or inability to act forcefully and decisively upon the environment. We turn our actions against ourself and avoid contacting its obstacles. In retroflection, the environment we act upon is us.

Where introjection and pseudoconfluence are disruptions of the early aspects of the gestalt process, projection and retroflection are disruptions that occur in its more advanced stages, when we have more clearly formed the figure/ground. The outcome of retroflection is often no action at all. We restrain our impulse, and the result is immobility. The immobility, though, is not resolution. It is the tension of opposites of equal strength working against each other. Physically, this is body armor, the constricted musculature. Emotionally, it may be seen in the counteracting of resentment by guilt, which again renders us inactive. Cognitively, it may be persistence of introspection countering and inhibiting our awareness; instead of contacting the environment, we contact our mentation.

Retroflection is a perversion of the golden rule. We do to ourselves what we want to do unto others. For example, we blame ourselves for the disappointments we have incurred as the result of the activities of other people. Or, angry, we bite off our nails instead of another's head.

We have seen that the disordering of health requires that the self be functioning in the aggressive style of the ego. This is clear in such operations as retroflection, introjection, and projection, but it is just as surely the case in pseudoconfluence, for the ability of the self to maintain itself in the style of the id in contraindication of the requirements of free functioning is an outcome of the self's ego mode. Only it is forceful and assertive; the id mode, by contrast, is accommodating.

This basic interruption of the figure/ground process, the forerunner of all impairments, is called egotism. Its healthy counterpart is self-conscious, willful, ego functioning. In impairment, it is deliberation used to annihilate ourself. Its satisfaction is in control, and in victory. Egotism is the common element in all the forms that our impairment takes. The satisfaction of egotism is different from the satisfaction of organismic self-regulation. Victory — making things as we wish them to be by overpowering the gestalt process — is not integrated behavior. Integrated, we are more playful and the result is resolution, not victory.

Egotism also gives us a false, deceptive sense of ourselves. We lose track of our exact proportions in relation to others and the natural world. We become arrogant, impressed with our own powers. In egotism, we lose touch with ourselves as part of the flow of life. We know mostly how we can control, manipulate, and overpower.

The result of egotism is that we place ourselves in the center of life. Pridefully, we make ourselves the measure of all things, a false humanism of isolation from the give and take of the field. We become rulers, and our domain is ourself and all we come in contact with.

All these types of contact are characteristic of abnormal functioning. Persisting, they become part of our second nature, our learned approach to our living that becomes so ingrained in us we feel it to be natural. Their variety permits us to interfere with the gestalt process at any stage of it. They can also be used in combination. We can, for example, project the introject that we should be refined and rational; then we will see our environment as controlled, and ourselves as out of control.

As long as we must minimize our excitement and our contact, these types of contact and engagement will be ours, for they are what we find it possible to do with reduced awareness. They are the adjustments we are structurally capable of, given the limitations we have set for ourselves. And we continue with them, because however unsatisfactory they may seem, we come to experience them and the experience they give us as us. Remember, in impairment we are always looking for ways to assure ourselves of our existence, and make things work out for us, and we do this by activities that promote our experience of our central importance in what we are doing. That is the essential aspect of abnormal functioning. Though they are learned and habitual behaviors and attitudes, we come to hold onto them and defend them as though they are vital organs, for they seem to stave off our destruction and reassure us of our existence. Because we are out of touch with the present, we continue to feel endangered. Because we are endangered, we cannot give in to the demands of the field and the emerging figure. So we hold on, control, and dominate ourself and the rest of the field.

Its evident irony is that by trying to make things work out, we ensure that they cannot. Seeking to produce our satisfaction, we frustrate ourselves. Attempting to exercise control over ourselves and the environment, we become uncontrollable. So, we come to experience ourselves as alien. We can't stop drinking or smoking dope, or eating, or thinking, or working. We hurt others, though we truly do not mean to, and we somehow cannot make ourself happy. We lose our temper, and we want everyone around us to put on a great big smile. We want everyone to be free like us, and we are willing to kill them if they do not want to be free like us, and even then we cannot make them. And, of course, we ourself are not free.

Disorders of the Self

In terms of the model of the self outlined in the preceding chapters, the initial phase of impairment that implodes our spontaneity distorts the modalities of the self and their interaction by cutting into our contact with the field. Instead of moving fluidly from one to the other, the result is that the self polarizes into the excitement of the id mode and the structure and deliberateness of the ego mode. The result is caricatures of these two aspects of the self — a distortion of our free functioning and a distortion of our deliberating — for both modes are transformed by being estranged from their normal intimate, balanced interaction. Instead of being indivisible components of a gestalt, distinct and yet integrated, they become set against each other. No longer alternative and coordinated modes of the self, they are its opposed parts. They become the self in conflict, impaired ego and impaired id functioning in contradiction.

Another way of understanding this important conception is to think of the self as composed of energy or excitement, and structure or form. They are the two sides of the coin that is our integrated self. One side, the id mode, is characterized by energy, flow, excitement, ease. Suggestively, it is passive, nature, passion, feminine, accommodating. The other side, the ego mode side, is characterized by structure, form, deliberateness. Suggestively, it is active, conscious, channeling, cognitive, masculine, aggressive, I-centered.

In healthy functioning, it is often impossible to separate their contributions. Nor would we want to, for that would misrepresent them by underlining their distinctiveness when it is their integration that is paramount in health. It is misleading here even to talk about these modes, for what we see and experience is simply changes in the quality of the functioning of the self. Sometimes — as in learning to paint or to drive a car — deliberation is more prominent; at other times — in dream and hypnagogic states, in dancing, in laughing — the loose excitement is more prominent.

That which keeps the self integrated is that which keeps us healthy: living in the present, in the now. Living in the now, our contact functions are adequate, and so all the pertinent parts of the field weigh in our experience and in the process of gestalt formation and destruction. It is this comprehensive contact with ourself and our environment that maintains the modes of the self in their harmony with each other. The situation controls.

The precondition for abnormality, then, is a loss of contact with the field, for just as contact unifies the self, lack of contact effects its disintegration. Contact is like gravity — it brings things into relationship. It centers and integrates them. Losing contact is like being in a gravity-free chamber, or driving on ice: a movement that would take us from the middle lane to the fast lane on the freeway sends us spinning around; trying to correct our course, we overcompensate, spinning in the other way when contact is diminished. Its modes — its directions — become exaggerated. We become grotesque, awkward, out of control.

Abnormality, by this understanding, is the malcoordination of structure and energy. Too much structure for the excitement is repression, deadness, stilted and formalized behavior; too little is impulse-ridden behavior, acting out, spacey, bizarre. And the greater the loss of contact with the field, the greater the malcoordination of the modes of the self.

At the extremity of the imbalance of the modes of the self, we see what are called schizophrenia and the psychoses, the more extreme disturbances. Their precondition is that our contact with the field by severely reduced. The given-ness of experience is annihilated. Instead, we are primarily in touch with our fantasies, thoughts, ideas, delusions — with the middle zone of our mental processes. This loss of contact makes possible a similar severe disruption in the coordination of the id and ego modes, provoking a tug of war with us as the battleground. One possible outcome is that in the altercation of the energy of our impulses and the strength of our determined will, our excitement outweighs our ability to restrain ourselves. We lose control. We cannot make ourselves do what we would like. We go as far as we can to impede our free functioning, but the pressure of our interference with our excitement is too great for the meager skills of our ego mode. By default, and since we are unable or unwilling to return to free functioning, the self's style becomes predominantly that of the id.

"In psychosis, the energy is unmanageable. Instead of being differentiated and distributed, it comes out in spurts." (F. S. Perls, 1969a, p. 135). With meager contact, the looseness of the boundaries of id functioning are exaggerated. Introjection, projection, confluence, the contact styles that depend on confusing ourselves and the outside can flourish. We should recognize in this a general description of aspects of the extreme disorders that are characterized by out-of-control behavior.

Other extreme disorders gain their primary characteristics from the same obliteration of reality and the nearly total domination of the self by the ego mode. We become "I"-centered to megalomania and paranoia, willful and deliberate to obsession and compulsion. Our boundaries are seemingly fixed, though our contact functions develop into delusions. We are not florid, but severe and controlled and poignantly, painfully self-centered. (Sometimes, as in hysteria, the modes of the self stay aligned to each other; here, contact with ourself is nearly obliterated, replaced by middle zone and outer zone contact.)

We should note here that these are not static states of being. As we struggle to find a better mode of functioning, we move between these different imbalances in the modes of the self. Our ability to make contact may alter somewhat, too, from time to time, allowing more unified behavior. While this does not mean a return to free functioning, it does imply that these states of abnormal functioning are not fixed or without some variation.

We should also note that functioning that is characterized by a preponderance of the id mode of the self is generally more extreme and more disturbed than functioning where the mode of the ego persists. Id mode dominance is more prevalent in extreme disorders than in ego mode dominance. In general, it seems that since a viable ego mode allows us to manipulate our contact with the field, we have more ability to moderate our dysfunction if our ego mode is well developed. Seen developmentally, the ego mode is a later occurrence in the growth of the self; so, in general, disorders in which the ego mode dominates indicate more balanced growth than disorders in which they take an inferior role.

For many of us, though, the farther reaches of disrupted functioning are background. In the foreground are the compromise stages, called "normality" and "neurosis," where we can look one way and envision our health, and look the other way and see these severe disturbances. Where we look from is our impasse. We partake of reality and of delusion. Our grip on what exists is not broken, though substantial aspects of the ground of being slip out from between our fingers. The ground of contact with elements of the field moderates the modes of the self and obliges their interplay. In general, the more contact with reality we have, the healthier we are; and the less adequate our contacting processes are, the more the modes of the self run loose in the company of our middle zone.

This may take the extreme forms found in what is called psychosis, or it may range through impairments that rob us of our lives but keep us out of mental hospitals and down to the disappointment and emptiness of normality and the unfinished business and dysfunctional behavior of the healthiest of us. No matter where we look on the continuum, the process of impairment is the same: an interaction of the disruption of our contact functions with the disruption of the modes of the self.

In the more moderate instances of our organismic dysfunction, the pattern is the same. To the extent that our ego mode is not capable of directing the excitement of the organism after it has interdicted our free functioning and distorted our contact, we are "impulse ridden," given to actions and statements that surprise us and seem inappropriate to others. We may be violent, "losing our temper" when things "get out of hand." We "act out" a lot, verbally or physically; our manipulative and expressive systems are out of touch with our centers, and our ego mode is not sufficient to contain the excitement of our unfinished business. On the other hand, if the ego mode is sufficiently developed so that we can largely effect our self-conquest, our spontaneous and inappropriate acts are minimized. Instead, we are inhibited, proper, and correct. Perhaps we act mentally, through fantasies and our ceaseless thinking. Useless thought, out of the process of gratifying our needs, is the only spontaneity we permit ourselves.

We can see that these poles still reflect the modes of the self; only the quality of the distortion is different. We are each of us likely to tend toward one or the other modes most of the time, depending on our backgrounds, capabilities, problems, and circumstances. Of course, these change — especially the last. And when they do, the balance of our inhibitions and our energy changes, too. If we are constricted, perhaps we become more so. We get uptight; or maybe we blow up, or go berserk, or freak out. If we are routinely dominated by our id mode functioning, a crisis is likely to increase our energetic and bizarre activity — or perhaps we will simply stop, catatonic. Nothing at all is better than chaos.

The Development of Impairment

For clarity, let us delineate the phases of the onset of impairment. We start with free functioning and the interaction between our impulses and acts and the environment. This is the level of contact, of authenticity and health.

The first stage of our impairment is when we mobilize ourself to maintain our ego mode functioning and use it to act against our own impulses, contracting against our moving out into the figure. At this point, we are armoring ourself to shield us from our urges. As part of this occurrence, we are cutting into our contact with the field by deflecting from our awareness anything that might further arouse us; we desensitize ourself. F. S. Perls called this the level of implosion. "The implosive level is where the energies that are needed for living are frozen and invested unused" (1970b, p. 241). We do this by freezing parts of our sensory and manipulative faculties into immobility.

The implosive layer is that level of reaction against the self. It is the point of self-alienation, where the ego mode imposes itself on the organism. As such, it is the point where we begin to treat ourself as an object. We make things out of our processes by doing things to ourself. Instead of being one with our bodies and feelings, we manipulate them to hold them in. By imploding ourselves, we try to cancel out our activity. Our free-flowing excitement is subjected to a kind of compression as we mount a defense against it. We are in conflict.

At this point we have countered the thesis of our spontaneity with the antithesis of our fear. Our moving out into figure formation is opposed by our self-restraints. In the development of impairment, the dialectic of spontaneity versus inhibition does not lead to a synthesis. Instead, we grind to a halt. The forces of our movement and restraint are counterpoised equally, like harnessed horses pointed in opposite directions. This phase of immobility is the impasse.

In the impasse there is little activity but much tension. Our excitement is focused in the conflict that renders us outwardly inert. We are locked here at the point of our conflict. We cannot go forward because we are afraid of the consequences, and we cannot go back because we have needs, desires, and interests that we wish to satisfy. This is the stuck point.

Though we find no way out of our impasse, we still have our life to live, so we make stop-gap solutions that permit us to function in some partial fashion. Besides, the impasse is an unpleasant place to be, full of tension, confusion, and frustration for us. Together these conditions provoke the level of functioning we create out of our impasse, the next phase in our impairment.

Remember, our impasse is the result of the unresolved conflict between our free-functioning concern for our needs and our appraisal of what we can do and survive. The first requirement of the level of functioning we construct for ourselves out of our impasse is that the impasse not be disturbed. Since it is such a difficult and debilitating experience to be in the impasse, we come to have a phobia about it. We begin to try to avoid circumstances, thoughts, and activities that will excite the elements of our conflicts, for if that happens, they will also excite their opposition and we will again find ourselves irreconcilably, painfully split.

The rationale of the next stage of our impairment is that it must distract us from the things that are most important to us. (That is what our unfinished business is.) In other words, the level of functioning we create to avoid our impasse is intended to be trite, dull, and meaningless, and at the same time it must allow us to manipulate the field in such a way that we do not confront our most pressing issues. We become phonies, and game players.

This phony, phobic level becomes the one we present to observers, and the one we try to live at. This is the level of playing roles without knowing we are players, and of controlling people and things. This is the level of playing games. At this surface stage of abnormality, there is little spontaneity, little genuine feeling, little contact. That is the reason for this layer. The point of this top layer of impaired functioning is to prevent authenticity, for that must unerringly lead to the resurgence of our conflicts. (At the same time, we will compound the artifice of this stage by masking our phoniness. We want to feel we are and appear to be genuine and spontaneous.)

Instead of dealing with our real conflicts, we create internal ones. Instead of solving real problems, we get involved with the fake ones we make. It is symptomatic of impairment that we are in conflict with ourselves. But at this inauthentic level of being, the conflicts we deal with are red herrings that draw us away from the empty, hopeless frustration and danger of the impasse. The purpose of false conflict is to avoid and interrupt the excitement of the emerging gestalt. As Freud said, "If you have two servants quarreling, how much work can you expect to get done?" (In Perls, 1951, p. xiii).

We blame ourselves or we blame others. We put ourselves down, or put others down. We feel alternatively resentful and guilty, sometimes righteous and sometimes sinful. We go around and around, to no avail and no end, for their intent is not to lead to any resolution of our distress. Our conflicts keep us from it, in our middle zone. Estranged from our contact functions, these polarities have no basis in our present needs or in the requirements of the situation. The conflict is pseudoconflict, a decoy. All the components of the would-be gestalt that never come to any resolution are creations of our middle zone. Our introjects conflict with each other, or with our conceptions of our needs. Nothing is real. On the battleground of our psyche, the mother we swallowed says, "You should not make anyone unhappy"; our idealized needs respond with childish petulance, "I can do anything I want." And on, and on.

Chapter 5

THERAPY: REINSTATING GROWTH

He could have cooked his rice much sooner.
It is too clear and so it is hard to see
A dunce once searched for a fire
  with a lighted lantern
Had he known what fire was
                    MU-MON, *The Gateless Gate*

Theories of change come from our understanding of what exists and what is possible. In the case of human events, they come from our understanding of the nature of human beings, the process of human growth, and the ways in which our functioning is disrupted.

In Gestalt therapy, we pay closest attention to the particulars of our existence, to the ways we are living our lives. Our observation is that our healthy functioning is disturbed by interferences with aspects of the gestalt process. Just as our original observations come from our interest in the process of being human, so does the framework for understanding and bringing about change. Now we come to describe the Gestalt method of restoring the organism to health: therapy is recovering the gestalt process and making us capable of free functioning.

In General

As we have seen, the primary interference with the process of our living is our diminished awareness. Awareness is our experience of what is happening to us, and the diminution of awareness impoverishes the gestalt process. All the abnormalities we discussed in the previous chapter stem from this initial impairment. Out of touch, we lose the ability to solve the problems of our living and find the satisfactions we need. The reader will recall that the persistence of dysfunctional crisis behavior long after it has any pertinence is the result of removing that behavior from our awareness by suppression and repression. The first step is to become aware of what we are doing to ourselves.

We have already seen that Gestalt therapy understands the free functioning organism to be capable of dealing adequately with the problem of living, provided that it is in full contact with those problems and its own possibilities for apprehending and organizing the field. The therapy consists of bringing us into closer contact with and greater awareness of the present.

To be aware of the present means that there is no longer any room for the middle zone system of delusions and distractions that characterizes impairment. To be aware of the present means that we are totally involved in each step of the unfolding pattern of fulfilling our needs that we call the gestalt dialectic. Therapy consists of learning to be aware of all the aspects of the gestalt process, from the undifferentiated field through the beginnings of destruction, through the polarizing of the elements of the field, through their unity in the new figure and its eventuation in making a new situation, and the final satisfaction and relapse into indifference.

To be aware of the present, to be totally in it, ensures that the self is functioning as it is meant to. The self is us, the accumulation of our experiences, our heredity, and our predispositions. As our awareness is enlarged the self comes closer to fullness and adequacy.

In Gestalt therapy, we do this by attending to how we go about living our lives. Therapy is an investigation of how we function in the world, and how we can function more in tune with our nature. It is first an inquiry into the ways in which we solve or fail to solve the problems we face, with the purpose of increasing our awareness of it, and then a careful experimental approach toward changing our functioning so as to make it more satisfying to us. In therapy, we examine the functioning of the self and create ways of increasing the scope and facility of its aspects.

> Quite briefly, my theory is the following. Difficult situations create wishful and magical thinking, scientific manipulation, propaganda, and the philosophy of the free will; in short deliberateness instead of spontaneity. Human behavior, in as far as it was objectionable to a person or a group, has to be changed, but the "goody-goody" behavior is not replacing, it is superseding the spontaneous attitude. Instincts as the source of unwanted behavior cannot be eliminated, only their expressions can be modified or annihilated. It is the expression and execution of the organismic needs, of the biological, original personality, which is paralyzed. Consequently, the modern individual has to be re-sensitized and remobilized in order to achieve integration.
>
> *(F.S. Perls, 1948, p. 570)*

The goal of therapy is to achieve enough integration so that we carry on the process of our own development by ourself. There is no way that conflicts can ever be resolved once and for all time, and Gestalt therapy does not require that we complete all the solutions we did not pursue to our satisfaction in the past. Therapy is successful when we are able to stay in touch with the field in emergencies and resolve them. The purpose of therapy is not to solve the problems of our living — that is the business of living. The point of therapy is to deal with our inability to deal satisfactorily with the circumstances of our life, and to discover the resources of our self, so that we can develop the new solutions we require to meet the demands of our needs and the environment.

The conflicts that are resolved in therapy are the conflicts within us, not those that in health form the substance of our lives. Inner conflicts are splits in the unity of the self, battles over who we are, what we are to do, and how we are to do it. When they exist, they make it impossible for us to grapple with real problems with facility. These are the reasons for the existence of Gestalt therapy, and it is limited to them.

This means the self is the focus of attention in Gestalt therapy. The workings of the gestalt process are what interests us in therapy. What is at issue is that, in impairment, we cannot coordinate the field so as to achieve gratification and achieve closure. Social norms and events are not dealt with in therapy, for they are not available to the process of therapeutic change. Nor are our natural processes available for alteration. As we have seen, they cannot be changed, but only accepted and accommodated, or constrained and overlaid. In fact, the goal, focus, and direction of Gestalt therapy is the integration of our instinctual functioning into our total organismic existence in the world.

As therapy unifies us, it frees the jailer and the prisoner. It releases the energy contained by all the parties to the conflicts within us, energy that can then be used in our lives. We have been our own oppressors, and the excitement of our spontaneous self has been locked into immobility or artifice by our fear. Therapy brings us back to life again. "Every credit is a debit, a transfer from somewhere. Nature does her bookkeeping by double entry" (Perls, Hefferline, and Goodman, 1951, p. 47).

Therapy is the process of learning to embrace ourself. In it, we try to replace our dreams and fantasies of living with total organismic functioning. To do that, we begin by embracing our present situation, difficult as that may be. In therapy, we face the facts of our lives that we have hidden from ourself. The task is to help us accept ourself.

"Change occurs when one becomes what he is, not when he tries to become what he is not." (Beisser, 1970, p. 77). To become what we are is to be aware of ourselves, now. Change is a function not of making ourselves different or resisting our impulses. It comes out of being fully ourselves. Things change as they are discovered. As we bring to our awareness what constitutes our existence at this time in our lives, we make change possible. The process of our living is one of continual change and growth. To be part of that process requires awareness of ourselves, contact with all the present moment of our existence. If we are awake and aware, we can grow and change. If we become aware that we seem to be incapable of finding an adequate solution, that awareness too is necessary for us to proceed to the elusive resolution of our difficulties. The awareness of being stuck, if it is total awareness, brings into being the new solution.

The process of therapy, then, is a process of enlarging our awareness, so that our natural functioning can reinstate itself. In this way we recover our free functioning.

There are two distinctive aspects to the therapy process: uncovering our present functioning and discovering ways to replace it with more adequate means of satisfying ourselves. The first aspect is attending to the phenomenology of our present behavior. We must first find out what it is that we have done to ourselves that constitutes our second nature of impaired functioning.

In this aspect of therapy, we get in touch with the unfinished business we have and with how we have held it in abeyance. The point of this is not to destroy our ability to exercise the kind of control we exercise over ourselves in impairment, but to make that control available to us so that we can choose whether to continue or alter it. Of course we know this self-control hinders our growth and satisfaction, and finding out about the means we use to make it happen will likely bring about its transformation. But that is not the intent of this aspect of therapy. It aims more modestly to give us custody over our acts and bring our self-conquest to our awareness.

Another way to think about this is to say that therapy intends first to bring us to an acceptance of ourselves. Its initial purpose is to restore to our awareness the attitudes and behaviors that constitute us at the present moment.

The intent here is to change only our awareness, not our acts. In fact we cannot find out what we are if we begin by changing them. We have also said, though, that restoring our present behavior to our awareness will result in a renewal of the gestalt process of change. And it will, for we usually find that what we are doing does not satisfy us, and our self-restraint against acting to form the figures we wish to form is not based on any present necessity. We find a disparity between the needs that are present in us — one pole of our inner conflict — and the ways we go about meeting them or failing to meet them. From this initial awareness of how inept we are, we come to begin to attempt to change our acts so as to make them more congruent with our needs.

Another frequent discovery in the process of enlarging our awareness is that we do not need what we thought we did. We find that our needs are simpler and more realistic than our frustrations have led us to believe. In other words, contacting our unfinished business does not necessarily turn us into ravenous gorgers, prey to our own appetites.

Much of what we find in this stage is that we have taken in "outside meddlers," social rules and familiar injunctions that we have laid over our own impulses without digesting them and transforming them and making them our own. We are obeying orders, doing what we are told, like good children. In general, we find that we are out of touch with our needs, and with the organism/environment interaction of the figure/ground process.

We can think of this therapeutic activity, literally, as brainwashing — or, as you would expect in Gestalt therapy, organism washing. By experiencing how we act, feel, and think, we begin to let go of the patterns of behavior and thought we have learned in adversity and gotten stuck with, and we begin to approximate the simpler process of organismic self-regulation. Ridding ourselves of our impediments to pursuing our interests, we are cleansed of our internal conflicts and self-defeating behavior. By attending to the phenomenology of our present acts, we begin to reassert our organismic control over them, and we are thus able to alter them to better suit us.

Another related aspect of therapy is trying out new modes of thought and action to replace the ones we begin to find unsuitable. Now that we have begun to interrupt our dysfunctional behavior, how are we to replace it?

We proceed by trial and error. We look to our self for the impetus to our new directions, and we try out the steps that go in that direction in therapy, finding successive increments of dealing with the field in the direction of our satisfaction. This is the experimental aspect of Gestalt psychotherapy.

The reader will notice that these two general facets of the therapeutic process are aspects of the gestalt process described earlier. Trial and error is an intrinsic element in the formulation of a figure, and present awareness is the adequate contact necessary for figure formation. In therapy, we are reinstituting our ability to form and follow our gestalts.

We should not conclude that these two aspects of therapeutic activity — contacting the present self, and inventing new behaviors — always occur in the order in which they were presented. Often, they do happen just as they were described, but that order is not inevitable, and the reader is urged not to conceive of neat and tidy resolutions to difficulties that have been arranged with such intensity, frustration, unhappiness, and tenacity. Therapeutic change is a cooperative activity where contact and invention interact to restore healthy functioning. It may happen in the order described above, or its reverse, or — more usually in the complexity of the actual process — in alternation and combination. We may, for example, attempt in fantasy to speak to someone who has intimidated us, out of a budding knowledge that we have in the past been afraid to say to them things we wanted to. But now, in the safe emergency of the therapeutic situation, our desire outweighs our fear. When we speak, however, we experience our words as vague, the tone of our voice as whiney and apologetic, and we notice our voice is muted and diffuse. So, we attend to our difficulties in speaking up for ourselves, and perhaps then we discover a more apt vocabulary. We may find out that we have held our breath as we spoke, and thus did not have the physiological support for our attempts. Perhaps we are able to breathe more deeply, and we try again.

In this example, we can see the alternation of contacting our actual behavior and inventing new ones through trial and error, and their interdependence and interpenetration. We begin by contacting our fear, come to wish to speak our minds — a trial solution to the frustration of our contact with the other — and contact again our experience of our speaking — the error, so to speak, of giving ourself inadequate support — then add to our first invention changes in our words and our vocal apparatus. Contact and invention interweave, born of each other.

Notice the intimate relationship between the structure of the behavior and its function. Attending to our speech, we change its form, making it more forceful and direct. Doing this we change its function — our contact is more energetic and arresting. We can describe the same alterations with a different emphasis: We improved our contact and clarified our needs by altering the form of our speech, deepening our breathing, and increasing the precision of our words. The first description emphasized the form of our alterations. The second emphasized their effect. Our point is that the function is changed when structure is changed, and we can alter the former to change the latter, or do the reverse. Change one, and we change the other. In therapy, we can attend to one or the other, since they are related in this way. (In the example above, we dealt with both, alternatively.)

In changing behavior to restore healthy functioning, Gestalt therapy is existential, experiential, and experimental. It focuses on us, and our relationship to the rest of the field. It is concerned with our awareness, our experience, our phenomenology. And its methodology for finding out how we are to change ourselves so as to better fit our needs to our desires is based on a playful manipulation of the field in order to discover what recourses will best meet the present problems and make for gratification. The goal of the therapy is to make it possible for us to form creative integrations of our experience in any situation and see them through.

Restoring the Ego Functions

Some aspects of this general procedure should be emphasized. Therapy does not consist only of discovering better ways of living. We cannot simply lay new patterns of functioning over old ones, anymore than we can build a new building without removing the old one. We must also dissolve the old gestalts. Much of our excitement is tied up in them, and the new solutions will not be adequate unless our resources are ample and unrestricted.

An important contribution of these procedures is that they redistribute the excitement that had previously gone in to the impairment. Remember that our functioning becomes impaired by our interference with free functioning. Our interference necessarily amounts to a two-step process. First, we replace the play of the aspects of the self with figure formation dominated by the ego functions. (How else would we insist on how we shall be?) Then, we avoid attending to this course of action and its consequences — awkward, inappropriate figures, or dull, graceless ones, or routine ones. We make the best creative adjustment which we can make and still avoid what seems intolerable to us, and then we distract ourselves from these pathetic accommodations. Finally, we forget.

In therapy our impaired functioning is undercut by the following recourse. Whereas the ego functions in abnormality force us away from those of our present awarenesses and needs which we feel we cannot confront, in therapy these same functions of the self redirect our attention back to the conflicts within us, channelling our awareness and excitement to our unfinished business. In order for us to reassert the healthy self-process, we must increase our contact with our present circumstances. We force ourselves to stand, look at and experience what we have been running from. The act — so basic to therapy — of dealing with our fears and our anxiety by attending to it, tolerating some amount of contact with unpleasant feelings, is the beginning of reestablishing the ego functions as a part of free functioning. The deliberate, forceful dimension of the self, itself so intimately involved in the origins of our dysfunction — is harnessed to achieve their dissolution. As our impairment developed, the ego functions were the weapons of our self-conquest. In therapy, they become one of the instruments of the restoration of the healthy self.

Therapeutic Style and Techniques

The surface of Gestalt therapy is the array of techniques popularized by its more dramatic advocates. Fritz Perls, especially, through his public appearances and the many films he made in the last years of his life, provided a vivid introduction to Gestalt therapy.

We should view the use of techniques of therapy in Gestalt therapy with these general attitudes. First, the Gestalt approach is a therapy. It is a pragmatic involvement with other human beings that intends to promote growth and development. Gestalt therapy is practical, and as it is practiced its emphasis is on therapeutic change. Gestalt is not primarily a philosophy or a life style, it is a therapy. So, in one sense it is perfectly apt to concentrate on its methods.

However, Gestalt therapy is done in as many ways as there are Gestalt therapists. The style of working that Fritz Perls developed and taught in his last years was his particular expression of Gestalt therapy. His style was formed out of some special circumstances. For example, Perls was to a great extent an apostle of Gestalt therapy. He wanted to spread the influence of Gestalt therapy. He performed in public settings and for general dissemination. What he did was to demonstrate Gestalt therapy. That was his stated intention; so, his work was dramatic, entertaining, and arresting. Further, Perls was a skilled public performer. He had acted professionally in his youth and was trained for theatrical work by Max Reinhardt. The particular style of his therapeutic work reflects his intentions, his training, and his preferences.

Perls said that reliance on techniques can impair growth. In Gestalt therapy, it is not desirable for therapists to learn techniques, to learn to do therapy like Fritz Perls, or like anyone else. What is essential is that the Gestalt therapist develop his own individual style of being a Gestalt therapist. To do that, he must chew it, break it down, take it in, and make it his own. For therapy to be entirely appropriate, it must respond as exactly as possible to the specific conditions of each therapeutic situation. So it will be different for each therapist, and with each patient, and different at each meeting. In Gestalt therapy, techniques are continuously invented. They arise out of the requirements of the therapeutic situation and are not fixed by prior practices.

In Gestalt therapy there is considerable emphasis on the development of style, not on the use of techniques. A style of therapy is a form of personal expression and communication that is integrated with the orientation toward being and growth that is the therapy's framework. In Gestalt therapy, styles of therapy spring from an apprehension of the mentality of Gestalt therapy. Or, more precisely, they come from the interaction between the therapist's skills and temperament and his understanding of the Gestalt approach.

Awareness

A methodology is a coherent group of methods, based on principles, by which an activity proceeds. The methodology of Gestalt therapy is those operating principles that support the particular expressions of Gestalt therapy that are each therapist's style. These principles of practice are drawn consistently from the theoretical outlines of Gestalt therapy that have been described in the preceding chapters — conceptions of health, of dis-ease, of how we move from the former to the latter, and how we can turn the tide.

The methodology of Gestalt therapy has as its immediate basis the theory of change outlined earlier in this chapter. Simply, it is that healthy organismic self-regulation is restored as the awareness of the organism is enlarged, for awareness moves it in the direction of its present needs. The prerequisite of the healthy gestalt process is awareness of and contact with the present system of needs and possibilities. Therefore, therapy consists of attending to present functioning and assisting us in discovering ways of increasing our awareness and contacting and manipulating the field based on the needs we uncover.

The kingpin of the Gestalt methodology is awareness. In therapy it takes the form of apprehending aspects of our experience. The task of therapy is to examine the structure of our experience, finding out what it is we experience, and how we do it. In contrast to approaches that are concerned with understanding *why* we behave as we do, Gestalt therapy is interested in finding out *what* we do, and *how* we do it. Introspection and an historical curiosity are replaced by an experiential examination of the structure and function of behavior. "To dissolve a neurotic system, one needs awareness of the symptom, not...explanations; just as to dissolve a piece of sugar one needs water, not philosophy" (F. S. Perls, 1947, p. 228).

For example, a patient expresses resentment against his wife for what he sees as a frivolous and wasteful use of money. The focus of the activities of the therapist is to mobilize all the patient's involvement in what he is doing. So, the therapist may ask that the patient notice how his resentment is experienced — in shallow, rapid breathing? clenched hands? a tingling in his arms? a tenseness in his shoulders? Perhaps the patient will be asked to express his resentment, and notice the form of the expression — is his voice soft or loud? whiney or apologetic or threatening? is he clear and direct? or diffuse and confused? or apologetic?

The purpose of these techniques is to bring our present existence to our awareness. By paying attention to ourself, we come to know what our actual experience is. This is a reversal of impaired functioning. In the latter, we are intent on avoiding aspects of our existence. In therapy, attending to our experience instead, we confront our life instead of avoiding it. In therapy, we encourage our health by being healthy. We move toward the goal of living in the present by living in the present and examining it, by being aware of ourself, our awareness, our situation, our existence.

It is not necessary to focus on experiences that are fraught with meaning or affect. We may just as well attend to seemingly elemental or even mundane aspects of our functioning, like the way we see, the way we chew, the way we walk. Each of these activities — parts of the continuum of our awareness and behavior — are elements of the whole that is each of us; thus, each activity will in some way reflect the whole. I recall requesting a patient to look at the doorknob of a closet door in my office. He remarked for some time, seated in his chair, on its objective qualities — color, shape, size — on "how it must be fastened to the door." He didn't test his opinion by going to the door and examining it more closely. He didn't express any feeling about it, or any interest. This is someone who keeps his world at arm's length, who speculates and does not get involved, and does things that don't interest him. His typical method of gestalt formation and destruction and his impairment of that functioning are apparent in this behavior.

In this kind of therapeutic work, we attend to the continuum of our awareness. We discover how we function in the world by staying with the changes in our present experience. What is current may be a crisis, or the heightened pleasure of sensuality, or sitting, breathing, looking, touching, listening. In all cases we come to the full realization of what we are at the present time by engaging at all the points on the continuum of our awareness.

Contacting the present in this way reduces the importance of the middle zone. The arena of subvocal speech, of useless concepts, memories, and anticipations is depleted as our awareness expands. Because of this, awareness itself is a propelling force for change. Reducing our involvement in our distractions, we become aware of the remnants of our unfinished business. Attending to the present reveals what we have been trying to distract ourselves from.

It should be clear by now that the methodology of Gestalt therapy has the same characteristics as have its theory of knowledge and theory of behavior. To focus on awareness means, again, that the here-and-now, our existence, and our experience are central. In Gestalt therapy, we are not historians, or symbolists. We are existentialists, phenomenologists, working in the present moment.

What is available in the present to the therapy is what we can be in touch with; our movements, gestures, speech, feelings, posture, our expressions, our interaction with reality. Working in the present, we deal with what is in front of us, the surface of behavior. This is one of the major characteristics of the Gestalt methodology, that it is oriented to the surface of behavior. It deals not with the deepest recesses of the unconscious but the obviousness of present functioning. "Obvious," from the Latin, and "problem," from the Greek, have the same root meaning: in the way. What is in your way is what is in front of you.

To attend to the continuum of awareness is to contact both ourselves and the world. The more we are aware of ourself, the more we contact the world, because discovering ourself opens us to new experiences. Conversely, the more we contact the world, the more we discover ourselves, for our apprehension of the field is an act of ours. Making contact with an other, we also discover that part of us that is contacting. We learn about our boundaries — the point of meeting and separation — and we learn our sensitivities.

Reactivating Aspects of the Gestalt Process

The dialectic of the gestalt process is, we have seen before, identical with the activity of the self. Thus, the development or redevelopment of aspects of that process is equivalent to strengthening and enhancing the self. Good present experience has intrinsic healing power. It heals because it is the regeneration of the process of living. Any activity that is healthy functioning is therapeutic, for it brings us back into contact with the elements of free functioning, beginning to renew our confidence in that process by contacting the present possibilities instead of our expectations and anxieties. Living in the present teaches us that our fears are unfounded, by showing us what is really us and what truly exists outside of us. With awareness, we replace the terror of the impasse with present, real, and circumscribed life problems — the constituents of the business of our living. With awareness, we begin to see the alternatives that are open to us, for we have reinstituted the process of the self.

The gestalt process is not a mechanical one. We can point to aspects of it, its ingredients and outcomes. We know that contact, involvement, and discrimination are facets of it, and resolution is its eventuation. But we don't really know its workings and cannot tamper with the basic process of gestalt formation. Bringing things together is magic. In therapy, we do not directly reform the figure/ground process; we cannot do that. It is an autonomous process, indirectly responsive to our ministrations. What we can do is to practice the initial parts of the process. We can develop the skills of contact, engagement, discrimination, manipulation, and in that way stimulate the process by allowing for the fullest exploration of the field. But the solution still comes, unbidden.

Support is essential for each new contact. Success in increasing and expanding our contact functions is based on support, and negative reactions and failure in making contact come from unsupported contact. To reach out to another and maintain our footing, our legs must be able to support us. To run, our lungs must be able to provide us with increased quantities of oxygen. To make love, our pelvic region must move fluidly, and we must be capable of contacting our lover, feeling her skin, his important caresses, her excitement, his desire.

Each incremental increase in our contact, each resurgence of healthy functioning, each successful contact episode becomes support for future contact and gestalt formation. As we integrate all our vital functions into our functioning, we increase our support for new contact. A history of successfully concluded gestalts is the support for taking new steps in awareness.

In Gestalt therapy, we are directly and centrally concerned with the appearance and expressions of emotions in the therapeutic situation. Emotions are, we have noted earlier, a major manifestation of organismic excitement and gestalt formation. The development of appropriate emotional expression an contacting present emotions constitute and important part of the therapeutic work. This is implicit in the methodological imperatives mentioned above. In Gestalt therapy, we are interested in the present experience of our feelings. If we talk about our feelings, the present experience is of talking about, not of feeling. So, in therapy we are interested not in reports about what has happened in the past, but what is happening now. If we were disappointed yesterday and we describe the incident in therapy today, our description is past tense, but our disappointment is not. The incident still has meaning for us, so our disappointment will be part of the description, and the therapy will concentrate on the feelings. The common Gestalt technique of restating past events in the present tense and requesting that the description be made as though the patient is experiencing it now for the first time brings the problematic past into the present. It becomes more clearly what it is, a present problem. A present problem is one that can be dealt with.

PATIENT: My mother called yesterday. She asked why I haven't written, and I got all choked up and stammered. I didn't know what to say. The rest of the conversation was the usual stuff — I'm a dutiful daughter. When I got off the phone, I felt sick.

THERAPIST: How do you feel now?

P: The same way. I'm queasy as I think about it.

T: Talk with your mother now. Let her start, asking you what she asked yesterday...

This time, the conversation between mother and daughter is monitored by the daughter/patient and the therapist.

T: What are you feeling?

P: I'm very tense; my stomach is churning.

T: Your breathing?

P: It's like I'm under compression.

T: Pay attention to how you compress your breathing.

P: (Pause) Oh.

T: What happened?

P: I was binding my stomach with my muscles. I realized I wanted to breathe more, so I did, and I felt a flash of tingling in my arms and head and I thought, "You stop making me feel guilty." I'm mad!

Dreams, fantasies, and unfinished business from our past are all dealt with in this same general fashion. They are with us as some present unfulfilled need. By bringing them as fully as possible into our present experience, we hasten their integration into our total functioning.

An effective and hence common technique for bringing past events into the present is to have the patient play the parts of the fantasy, dream, or memory. Investing them with our current interest and excitement enlivens them, so that their importance to us becomes clear and they can make their contribution to the coming gestalt. Playing ourself and the boss who has been giving us a hard time, we get in touch with what we have been afraid to say and do. We discover ourself.

P: I dreamed I was in a car, driving very fast — too fast — on a winding road.

T: Be the road.

P: I am the road. I am demanding and difficult. If you are careful and stay in touch with me, I will support you. If you go too fast, you will lose me and get hurt.

T: Be the car.

P: I am the car. I am excited by the speed I am moving at, but I am also afraid. I am not in control, and Jack is pushing me too far.

T: Be you, the driver.

P: I am trying to get somewhere, and this road is making it hard for me to go very fast. I don't like that.

The therapist has the dreamer engage these parts, and as they speak with each other, they come to appreciate their differences and to find some way to exist together. The road has more to offer than a way to get from one place to another. "I have vistas and surprises," it says. But it insists: "I cannot be straight. I am what I am. If you are on me, you have to follow my curves." The car speaks of its loyalty, service, and capabilities, and says it will be supporting of Jack if its limits and assistance are respected. The driver begins to appreciate these parts — parts of himself, for it is his dream — he has been estranged from. Working out the dream, he sees he has been fixed on the future and his desires, and he has missed what is around him. The car is his support, and the road is the reality of what he is engaged in. The dream is advice to him: Stay in touch with what you can do, and what is possible, as well as what you would like. These insights come to him as part of the dream work in therapy, with the vividness and directness that come from self-discovery.

Gestalt therapy is oriented to crucial emotional experiences because they are important to us. An emotion is a focusing of our excitement in such a way that our experiences have meaning. Emotions are the meaning of our experiences. Gestalt therapy encourages experiencing and expressing intense emotions, because they make our existence understandable and satisfying. We must abandon ourselves to them if we are to embrace all of ourselves, and if we are to come to workable solutions.

We are not talking here about catharsis, vomiting up emotions to "ventilate" us. "Nature is not so wasteful as to create emotions to throw them away" (F. S. Perls, undated c, p. 4). Emotions are an intrinsic part of experience, and it is necessary for us to recover them in therapy if we are to reorganize our excitement and gratify ourselves. We emphasize the emotional aspect of experience as part of contacting the totality of our lives. Our satisfaction requires that we express ourselves adequately, commensurate with our feelings, and that our feelings be part of the mix out of which will emerge new solutions.

In Gestalt therapy, the outcome of therapy is to be open to them, to let them be as a valuable and irreplaceable part of our experience. If we minimize them (or any of the other components of our experience), we diminish our lives. If, in attempting to find some resolution to our conflicts, we shy away from some of the ingredient difficulties — our shame or our fear, our anxiety or anger — we lessen the conflict, but we also lessen the usefulness and satisfaction of the solution. Though they seem to be threatening to us, staying in touch with the elements of our experience acts to strengthen the self, not to destroy it. Anxiety, pain and fear nourish us, if they are allowed to be part of our experience, for our contact with our emotions is part of the free functioning of the self. Involvement in our own lives keeps us grounded and centered in the facts of our existence. That is security.

Developing Discrimination

The aspects of methodology described above address the reconstitution of the contact, engagement, expression, and manipulation aspects of the gestalt process. Another methodological focus is on the discrimination necessary for good functioning. In order to organize the field accurately, with subtlety, refinement, and the most suitable materials, we must be capable of making distinctions. We must know what is us, and what is not us, what is past and what is present, what is pertinent to our present needs, and what is not.

Many awareness techniques are designed to refine our discriminatory processes. We may ask a patient to voice his fantasy of what another person is thinking about him. If the latter person is present, as they might be in group or family therapy, we may ask the other to say what he is thinking. If he is not present, the patient may be asked to role-play the absent other. In this way the patient can experience his expectations and then, in contrast, contact the other.

P: If I said that I wanted to live alone, my mother would be hurt.

T: How do you know?

P: I don't, I've never tried. But that's what I think would happen.

T: Let's check it out. Are you willing to experiment?

P: Yes.

T: Okay. Start with where you are; tell your mother what you want.

P: Mom, I know you won't like this, but I want to live by myself. You know I'm old enough, and it's safe, and I need to run my own life more.

T: How do you feel?

P: A little shaky. My breath is fast and fluttery; my voice is kind of...forced.

T: Can you say something about what you're feeling?

P: Yes. I'm afraid to ask you, but I am glad to, also.

T: Fine. Now, be the mother in you, your mother as you know her.

P: Hm. Well, I have a lot of feelings. I admire Jean's standing up for herself...

T: Speak to Jean. Make contact with her.

P: Yes. Jean, I'm glad you can say that. I feel a lot of things now — I admire you for wanting to step out on your own. I didn't ever do that. I also wish you wouldn't, for my sake. I like having you at home, seeing you grow, and keeping me company. I could be angry at you for leaving me alone, but right now I'm not.

T: What was that like?

P: I didn't expect what I said, really, and I don't know if she will respond as I did when I played her. But I really felt her love for me and how she is trying to take care of me. I also felt her sadness, and some bitterness about not having enough in her life...

Experiments in discrimination may be concerned with us and our contact with the environment, as in the above illustration, or with our contact with ourself. We may listen to different sounds, gaining experience in grasping what is different about them. What is it about my voice that distinguishes it from yours? What is its volume, pitch, melody, timbre, resonance, articularity? Or we may learn to refine our sense of our own emotional reactions, so depression and sadness come to be distinct experiences, and irritation becomes something other than rage. We must become able to know the differences in what we contact, for if we do not, the crudity of our contact will be reflected in crude experiences, and the activity that results from our contact will result in either vague, inept, or unsatisfactory solutions. Without refinement in the aspects of the gestalt process, we will not satisfy ourselves, for our needs are more specific. To finish our depression, we must start by expressing our resentments; to finish our sadness, we must mourn. One activity cannot replace the other.

Characteristic of impairment is the substitution of synthetic internal problems for real problems in making a creative adjustment in the environment. If I say I don't like your cooking, I make you feel bad, and then I feel guilty; if I don't I feel bad, irritated and out of sorts, and I withdraw and sulk. Another part of the methodology of Gestalt therapy relating to discrimination attempts to bring these internal conflicts into the present. Identical with the playing out of dreams, unfinished life situations and fantasies, we role-play each of these internal voices, making an intrapersonal encounter out of that endless argument.

Taking both sides of the argument, we allow both parts of us to develop fully. Each pole gets its full recognition as we take responsibility for them in this role play.

P: I don't want to tell Steve I'm leaving. It would hurt and upset him.
   But I am miserable with him.

The therapist directs the patient to be each of these parts of her, and to make them talk to each other.

P: You don't care about Steve. You are selfish.
   You don't care about yourself. You'd rather make yourself miserable than him.

P: Look, you just want to have a good time. You just want to take care of Mrs. Perfect, and not — you just don't want to put yourself out, to love Steve.
You're right, I know. And I feel really rotten. I feel selfish and greedy. But I really have trouble doing it. I'd like to be more giving to him, but...

The therapist asks the patient to observe and report on what she is aware of inside herself.

P: I feel kind of dull. Dead. Nothing there.

T: How do you experience that?

P: My shoulders are tense, my breathing is very shallow. My stomach is hollow — well, not really, there are kind of tickles of feeling there.

T: Be those little tickles.

P: I am life. I am alive. But she keeps me down.

T: Who are you talking to?

P: My stomach muscles, actually.

T: Tell that part of you directly, then.

P: Let go, stomach. You're killing me. I need room to breathe, to move.

T: Respond, now. Be Sheila's stomach muscles.

P: I'm a little afraid of you. Of what you will do. But I didn't know I was holding you down. I want to give you room. I'll try to.

T: How will you do that?

P: Breathing more.

T: Yes. Take some deep breaths.

P: That's much better. I feel more alive, and relaxed.

T: Anything else going on?

P: Yes. I am angry. All that stuff about just loving him and letting him walk on me makes me mad.

T: Go on with the dialogue, then. Tell that to the other part of you.

P: Look, that makes me mad. I love Steve. But I won't break my back — break my soul for him. It isn't — no relationship is worth my hurting myself like that. Like you do.

T: Respond.

P: Just what I thought. You're selfish, egocentric.

Attending to the process, the therapist points out the quality of blaming and rancor in the interaction. "Yes," replies the patient, "we're really at swords' points."

T: How do you feel about that?

P: I don't like it. I'm tearing myself apart...You know, I'm forgetting things, too: that I can be caring and also care about myself.

T: Ah. Continue with the dialogue, then.

P: I can be caring of Steve, just as you are. I love him, but I want to love myself, too. *And* I want to love myself, too.

Staying in contact with the conflict, the interaction moves from blaming to mutual understanding.

P: I feel like all I am is caring for Steve, sometimes. Like I would do better if I had something else besides that — more caring for myself. I don't give myself enough credit.
And I have been so busy doing that, I forgot I love him.

This duality has come close to a healing solution the unified self can accept. The resolution was made possible by accentuating the split. It is when internal differences are drawn to their clearest distinction that accommodations can emerge that are suitable for both parties.

Polarities in Therapy

Notice that the split which was developed in the preceding example is a polarity. As we saw in an earlier chapter, the process of making distinctions within the field is often one of separating into opposing poles. Here, one pole of the patient is her "selfishness" and the other pole is characterized by not taking her own interests into account.

Earlier, we said that polarities are often artificial problems. In this example, we can see how that is so. The patient defined her difficulty so that it set two aspects of her relationship to her lover against each other and then she kept trying to oblige herself to choose between them. Either she could respect her own needs or she could love him. We can see how this endless internal conflict cuts into any efforts she might put into the real difficulties of working out a satisfying relationship with her lover.

This example touches on another important area. Gestalt therapy is largely a way of understanding our behavior and interaction which stresses process. If we were to separate behavior into the components of form and content, Gestalt therapy concentrates on the form or structure of behavior. We are, for example, more concerned with the dialectic of polarities — how polarities form and are dissolved — than we are in the particular kinds of polarities which occur. To take a familiar example: the oedipus complex is a way of referring to a recurrent pattern of family interaction which often occurs during the formative years of a child. The oedipus complex is a generalization about the content of those interactions, and a major insight of psychoanalysis is that the particular elements of family interaction which taken together are called the oedipus complex represent one of the favorite patterns of relating between parents and children. The group of behaviors which make up the oedipus complex are, in Gestalt therapy, considered in relation to a different set of generalizations — ones about contact, gestalt formation, the boundaries of the self, and so on. What is important to us is not so much the recurrence of the parent and child striving and confusion in the areas of affection, power, and sexuality. These are issues of content, like the story line in a novel. They are basic to many theories of human behavior, but as we have seen, they have played practically no part in our explication of Gestalt therapy. Instead we pay attention to variations in contacting, in the functioning of the modes of the self and in the relationship of each party's contact with the actual present situation.

There is a major exception to this stance, and it is illustrated in the last example. One part of the patient says, "Look, you just want to have a good time...you just don't want to put yourself out for Steve." The other pole says, "You're right, and I feel real crummy. I'm bad, selfish, greedy."

We recognize this as a familiar split within ourself. There is a part of us which is trying hard, but doesn't quite succeed. We try to lose weight, to be on time, to stop being irritable, to spend more time with the children or less time with them, to study more, to be responsible, to be adult — but try as we may, we usually don't make it. In Gestalt therapy, this part of us is referred to as the underdog. The underdog says, "You're right. I'm wrong, I'm bad, I'm inadequate, I'm incompetent. Don't be mad at me, I try. I really do. But somehow..."

The other side of the polarity is the top dog. Our top dog says, "Lose weight! Be on time! Be responsible!" It says, "You are stupid and unreliable. You should be reliable." Our top dog is nagging, blaming, demanding, self-righteous — the stereotypic harsh parent. It cannot be satisfied for long, but prods us to live up to its standards.

Therapeutically, the top dog/underdog polarization is dealt with like any other polarity. Typically, as the top dog is more fully developed, its predominant qualities are augmented by the addition of frustration and helplessness, for the top dog is usually the loser in this intrapersonal conflict. Developing the pole of the underdog, its self-denigration, helplessness and acceptance of the standards of the top dog turn to sabotage, then to overt defiance. "No, I won't do what you want. I'm tired of your nagging, your shoulds and demands. I want freedom from you." The poles become more nearly equal, their opposition heightened. It is at this point, when the thesis and antithesis of the dialectic have both been realized, that this longstanding internal conflict can move forward toward unity and integration.

Experiment: Increments of Change

In the discussion above, we have emphasized the importance of aspects of Gestalt methodology concerned with awareness. They form the base line for the experimental aspects of the methodology. Often we find that we are not in touch with aspects of our functioning. We have scotomas, blind spots in our awareness. Perhaps we discover that we do not look at the eyes of others, or the breasts of women, or we do not hear much at all. Perhaps we find our rib cage and chest are always tense, and our breathing is never deeper than our stomach.

At this point, the direction of the therapy takes the form of graded experiments designed to increase awareness. For example, the patient may be asked to tell his father in fantasy what he has told the therapist: He resents his father for permitting his mother's hysteria relationship to the patient, as a child, without protecting him. Perhaps the patient is unable to do that. He says, "I can't." The therapist pursues his resistance to the experiment, asking him to enlarge upon his "I can't." The therapist may point out that he is capable of voicing his resentment, and "I can't" expresses helplessness. He is saying he is incapable of voicing his resentment.

The therapist has made the patient aware that he is capable of speaking his resentment to his father, but he has expressed his incapability. Perhaps he can, but is unwilling. Perhaps the patient then accepts that, saying, "I won't. I won't tell him I am angry at him for leaving me at my mother's mercy. He never listens." This is already an important step. The patient has taken responsibility for not contacting his father. He has established his own authority over this act, and learned some aspect of the generality that he is living his life — it is not just happening to him.

Therapy is a safe emergency. It is safe because it is structured with the patient's interests in mind, because it is not the real life danger — after all, Father is not present — and because the patient can leave. It is an emergency because its experimental orientation requires that what occurs in therapy is both within the range of possibility for the patient, and also real and challenging enough to arouse the conflicts that make his present life situation untenable.

Experiments are not tasks. Their point is not to get them done. They exist in Gestalt therapeutic work to provide present information about the patient. What happens if you do this, or that? The importance of experiments is in how they permit us to examine what we do, and to find out what we will not do. What we will not do is our resistance, our reluctance or felt inability to carry out experiments. Seen in this way, our resistances serve as much of the stuff of the therapy, for they are expressions of how we hold ourself back. What, for example, is going on with the man above is that he cannot, in a room where only he and his therapist are present, pretend to say to his father that he resents him.

In Gestalt therapy, the experiment has the methodological centrality that interpretation has in psychoanalysis and dream analysis has in analytical psychology. In the experiment, the patient permits his organismic self-regulation to begin to try to operate in the safety of the therapeutic situation. The experiment is the means whereby we run our organismic demands up against the limitations we have imposed on our self-functioning.

In skillful therapy, the experiments are ordered so that every trial brings both successes and new resistance. Each experiment has within it the potential for coming to grips with an aspect of our self-conquest in a setting where we may again begin to assert the predominance of our present satisfaction over outmoded ways of being. Action leads to feeling, feeling to understanding. In the experiment, we come to know what we do, and in the process, we discover new paths.

This experimental orientation is not the same as simply applying techniques. It consists of discovering the particular kinds of experiments that will enable this person to take the next step in his development. The patient is required to explore difficult avenues of his behavior with whatever venturesomeness he can muster and in full confidence of his trepidations. But the experiment must be safe enough to allow him to chance being open to altering and relaxing the dysfunctional attitude with which he habitually meets this situation. He must try to replace some part of his control and deliberation with the excitement and contact of his free functioning, so something new can come of the experiment.

No program of techniques can be matched to these demands and fit well enough to be useful. Experiments must be and are designed ad hoc to take the patient in steps from where he is when he enters therapy to a point where he can carry on the business of life by himself. The therapy begins where the patient is. Gradually, in steps small enough to ensure he can make them from where he is, and with what support he has and has developed, he moves toward his potential, to spontaneous behavior.

Resistance, Risk, and Frustration

We have remarked earlier on the origins of our resisting. They are in our ego mode's imposition on free functioning that persist because we lose track of what we are doing, or because we feel we are still endangered. Resistances are originally valuable aspects we developed to meet felt needs. Recontacting them in the therapeutic work is valuable because we rediscover parts of our functioning we had lost. To rediscover them is to find part of ourselves.

We recontact resistances not to remove them, or to overpower them. For some of us a major sense of our capabilities and our needs has come from saying no. On the other hand, resistances as unaware behavior keep us out of the present, and thus they make it difficult for us to take care of our needs. What is necessary is that they be brought to our awareness. We get in touch with our resistance so that the act of saying no is felt by us to be part of the process of our living. At that time, we may choose to try some other way to lead our lives, or we may not. Only if we have that choice are we responsible for ourselves.

As it is usually used in psychology, "resistance" has some implications which are not part of the Gestalt approach. We have already seen that resistances are not simply undesirable or neurotic traits; rather, they are gestalts formed in straitened circumstances. As the results of prior figure formation, they are integral parts of our functioning created to help us meet situations in what seems to us to be the most adequate fashion.

In the context of therapy, "resistance" is often used to suggest that the patient is resisting the therapist as he tries to do therapy, and that the patient's resistance is obstructive, wrong, or bad. Instead, we understand the statement that a patient is resistant as meaning that the patient will not do what the therapist wants him to do. That is, it is a statement about the therapeutic relationship from the point of view of the therapist.

In Gestalt therapy, resistances are the central focus of the therapeutic work, since they are the place where the patient demonstrates interference with free functioning — and at the same time demonstrates aspects of himself that are basic to him.

The patient is being what he is; the point of therapy is to bring that to his awareness. Resistances are opportunities for enlarging the patient's awareness to include his unwillingness or felt inability to experience something. From this standpoint, Gestalt therapy can be understood as a continuing examination and development of resistances, though it is equally accurate to say that in Gestalt therapy there are no resistances — who or what would the patient resist? — simply the experience as it unfolds.

Resistances reveal themselves in our difficulty or unwillingness in doing an experiment, and in the interruptions of our contact and concentration while doing it. We may become tired or bored, or restless; we may be overstimulated or understimulated sensorily, seemingly unable to respond to sensations, or overly excited to displeasure, disgust, or fear. These resistances evidence a present interference with our functioning.

P: I am having difficulty concentrating on the dream scenes I was describing.

(The dream is concerned with the patient's relationship to her dead mother.) The therapist asks her to elaborate on the difficulty.

P: I feel distracted, the scene seems very far away. I am aware of my breathing, which is shallow and a little fast, and my hands are holding one another.

Requesting that she continue to attend to her present experience, the therapist is allowing the patient's self-regulation to assert itself. (Remember, what she is doing — her boredom in this instance, and in the large case the dissatisfactory behavior that brought her into therapy — is the best she feels she can do. It is organismic self-regulation tied to her interests, in a field where her interests are bound up with many restrictions.)

P: I feel upset. My shoulders and chest are tight, tense, and my eyes ache a little, like I want to cry.

The therapist asks if she does, indeed, want to cry, and the patient admits that she does, and at the same time is afraid to. Is she aware, then, of keeping herself from crying.

P: Well, my cheeks feel very hard, like my jaw is clenched. It is. And I feel the tightness in my chest stops me, too.

The patient is asked to experiment by relaxing her jaw and changing her position so she can breathe more deeply. She agrees to do this, and as she does, she begins to weep. In the weeping, she discovers she is crying the mourning for her mother that she did not do when her mother died.

Making contact with these surface manifestations of present functioning, we come eventually to the center of important business — like pulling the little red tab on a package of chewing gum opens the whole package.

Like this example, most instances of resistance are issues of the body. Resistances are muscular tensions by which we restrain ourselves. We are holding ourselves in. Resistances are retroflections on the level of our bodies, ourselves squeezing ourselves. Much of the therapeutic work is therefore necessarily concerned with our bodies. We must begin to become aware of the ways in which we impose on ourselves; then we can, if we wish, use all that energy in the one direction of gestalt formation, rather than splitting it into opposing forces that reduce us to impotence. We must come to reown the muscles we have used to restrain ourselves, so that we can become free to use them as we wish — to restrict us if that seems best, or to assist us in finding new and more satisfying ways to live.

The example above is noteworthy in other aspects. First, it again instances the importance of forceful and resounding emotional experiences in the course of therapy. They indicate that the therapy is concerned with issues of moment to the patient, for strong emotional expressions come about when we care deeply about something. After all, it is the accumulation of these issues that brings us to therapy. If the time and struggle is to be worth the candle, the work must bring us to some resolution of them.

Another important part of Gestalt work revealed in this example concerns the importance of tolerating and staying in contact with difficult and demanding situations — in this case the anxiety and fear that were the preliminaries to the resolution of the patient's dream work. Here we can see the ego mode of the self being used in the service of her growth, using the discipline that is healthy retroflection in order to stay with what is developing out of the dream material. This is part of the hard work of therapy, demanding of ourselves that we make and endure contact with unwanted and unpleasant emotions. It is also the risky aspect of therapy, for while we are experiencing emotions that we have tried to avoid in the past, only the safety of the therapeutic context serves to assure us we will survive this encounter with our pain. To succeed in therapy, we must be willing to take these risks and make what is unpleasant part of our life. Once we have done this, once we have met ourself in these intrapersonal encounters, we can begin to transform ourself and leave what we have been afraid of behind. This process is the road to health.

We have seen earlier that a constant undercurrent of abnormal functioning is its infantility. Usually from long habit, we try to bypass steps of the gestalt dialectic, manipulating the environment so it will take care of us instead, or simply refusing to get involved in the sometimes arduous business of finding out what we need and what is available, contacting the relevant parts of the field, and creating a new and satisfying situation out of it. This behavior is infantile and regressive because we try to have others do for us what we are capable of doing for ourselves. We are acting like children. It is part of our second nature, and so we carry it into the therapeutic situation.

Another of the risks of therapeutic work that must be skillfully modulated by the therapist is the frustration that ensues when it becomes clear to the patient that he, the patient, is going to have to take care of his unfinished business. The therapist will not do it for him, and it will not magically happen.

"I've been very unhappy in my work for a long time, I'm thinking of leaving it. What do you think, doctor?" A typical, difficult life situation. But there is nothing helpful in giving the patient a solution to it. The business of therapy is to frustrate that dependency, making the patient aware of how he short-circuits developing his own skills by asking others to solve his problems. At the same time, the therapy must begin to help him contact his own needs and resources. These must happen together, or the frustration only leaves the patient with less than he started with.

If a solution is to be therapeutic, it must not only deal adequately with the given problem, but also be an instance of the patient discovering that he does in fact have what he needs to create that solution. Skillful frustration in therapy forces the patient to mobilize his energy in some other way than toward trying to make others lead his life, or into being depressed, or unhappy, or confused. For the frustration in this case is blocking the normal avenues of escape from his existence in such a way that the patient's impetus is redirected toward finding new ways of coping.

Spontaneity and Pseudospontaneity, and Concentration

It is important to distinguish spontaneous healthy functioning from mere physical spontaneity. The latter, usually referred to in psychology as "acting out," is the expression of one of the poles of our internal conflicts. It is not health. In impaired functioning, most of our behavior is acting out. Even when it is socially acceptable and moderated, it is a pseudospontaneity, an expression of one of the places where we have gotten stuck. Most instances of violence against ourselves and again at others are acting out our conflicts. But so, all too often, is the discipline of public-school teachers, the enforcement of public law, child rearing, the administration of public policy, and the waging of war. Disordered, we can only act out, for we are not acting from our center. We do not have the support of contact with the processes of the self and the environment that is the requisite for integrated behavior.

Acting out is sometimes encouraged in the experiments of therapy, in order that we become aware of what we do, or what we wish to do. Acting out promotes contact with the roles we play and shows us the scope of the excitement we have available to us. In this way, we can begin to take responsibility for the impulses we suppress and for our present behavior. Getting in touch with our current existence, we can then move to a new place.

P: I feel very angry. I realize he has left me to do his dirty work. Joanne is his friend. Let him entertain her.

T: How do you feel your anger?

129

P: My voice has gotten loud. My fists are clenched, my arms are itchy, my breath is deep and fast. Wow — I don't feel tired any more. I could slug him — and he makes fun of women for being helpless. I could kill him. Oh!

T: Tell him. Talk to that pillow as though it were he.

P: You fucker. You bastard. I want to...(She pummels the pillow for a time).

T: What's going on?

P: Well, I feel terrific. Boy, I didn't realize I was so pissed off at him. And also...well, I won't go kill him, but I sure need to straighten this out.

Authentic spontaneity is not easily won. "We can become spontaneous only by utmost discipline" (F. S. Perls, 1970b, p. 34). In Gestalt therapy, we gain our free functioning by experiments and investigations of our awareness and expression. The techniques designed to increase our contact stimulate the gestalt process that is the spontaneous functioning self.

Therapy is a demanding and disciplined endeavor for therapist and patient. In Gestalt therapy, we get to the spontaneity of the self by the discipline of attending to the continuum of awareness. We pay attention to our experience. This activity is called concentration.

What is now called Gestalt therapy was at one point in its history to be known as concentration therapy. Its use as a psychotherapy is based on the process of single-minded attention to the structure of impairment and the awareness of our functioning. Concentration is the act of focusing our consciousness in what is happening with us. All the aspects of Gestalt methodology described above require the exercise of some form of concentration.

Concentration is one of the attributes of the functioning of the self that in the ego mode plays a large role, and in the id mode plays a lesser but still important one. It is a willful activity, the channeling of energies of the organism to one part of the field, a focusing of attention that is both loose and alert. Concentration is not a rigid, fixed stare, paying attention in spite of ourself as we did when our teachers or parents said, "Pay Attention!" It is rather a relaxed attending — gentle, not grim, the easy pervasiveness of land fog. It is not less demanding because it is relaxed. Perhaps it is harder, a little like the injunction "Relax!" What is required is that we be able to observe our own activity and experience, staying in touch without crushing what is happening by our attention to it.

In therapy, this facility is utilized to direct our excitement to our unfinished business. Gestalt therapy stresses the importance of spontaneous behavior. The acquisition of spontaneity is, however, the result of the concerted application of our awareness.

In the context of the entire therapeutic process, spontaneous free functioning is gained by the coordination of the discipline of our concentration and the permission we give ourselves to be as free as we can. Experiments are acts that we attend to as thoroughly as we can, so that we can take the experience of them into ourselves and use it for our growth. This combination is in a way paradoxical — health gained through both intent and freedom — but it is very much the same combination as the relationship of the modes of the self. Just as the process of free functioning is a complex interaction of our assertion and our acquiescence — give and take — joined to a single purpose, the therapeutic process requires the same intersection of intention and abandonment. In the therapeutic method itself is the germinal activity of the dialectic of the gestalt process, the way of our living.

Congruence

P: Boy, I feel funny today. My boss really gave it to me yesterday. I guess...well, if it made a difference I would be upset.

T: What are you feeling now?

P: My arms are tight. My right hand is in a fist. I am so angry at him I could scream.

T: Are you aware of your voice?

P: Yes. It is very even, kind of a monotone. Trembling a little, too. It doesn't sound angry.

T: I don't sound very angry. What is your objection to expressing your anger?

P: I feel like I'd blow up this room, demolish you...No, I don't. I am so angry I could scream!

T: Again.

P: I AM SO ANGRY I COULD SCREAM. I am. That's where I am.

Out of our foundation in holism comes the therapeutic emphasis on developing ourself so that all the components of our experience and expression are unified. When we are one, we are ourself. We become one by putting all of ourself into each activity, each moment, every meeting, every experience. In therapy, we round up the stray elements of ourself and are reunited.

The Use of Language as an Aspect of Therapy

Language is an important part of the contact we make with others. Used with directness and precision, it permits us to communicate ourself. In Gestalt therapy, great attention is paid to the language as an aspect of our comprehension and expression of our lives.

The terminology of Gestalt therapy has been chosen to be for the most part closely tied to the processes of our experience, in order that how we talk about what happens with us and the events themselves are closely linked. Categorization is avoided, and behavior is usually referred to by phrases from ordinary language. We talk about "contact" and "withdrawal," of "needs," "support," and "spontaneous behavior." (Gestalt is not simon pure in this regard, as witness "confluence," retroflection," and "introjection." But the more abstract technical terms are almost never used in the course of therapy, only in discussions such as this.)

Popular speech contains many instances of wisdom that has been gained over many generations and that, sometimes unwittingly, gives us key insights into the experience of another person. We say that a person who is irritating to us is "giving us a headache." And, sure enough, many physical disorders — pains in the neck, in the head, in the ass — emanate from constraining our expression. But the point here is that what we say and how we say it can convey important information about us.

The forms our language expressions take are often symptomatic of our general attitudes and beliefs. So, we say, "It is painful to think about my children," when we mean that we feel pain. "It is painful," is a common convention of our language, but it also expresses our estrangement from our feelings, individually and collectively. We say, "I have a pain in my stomach," as we say, "I have an arm." These expressions are parallel to saying that we have a house, or a car, or an appointment. In speaking this way, we make emotions and feelings into accoutrements, ever so slightly but significantly removed from our being.

There are some general approaches to the use of language in therapy. First, there is a constant striving to develop a facility of expression and a vocabulary sufficient to reflect the depth and variety of our experiences. This task goes hand in hand with other therapeutic activities so that the creation of an expressive style that reflects what is happening with us comes at the same time as we become aware of increasing subtleties of experience.

"When I saw my son swat our dog, I saw red."

The therapist asks the patient to elaborate on his experience, to draw out the different strands of his reaction. Eventually, he says, "I got a big knot in my stomach, as though my hands were holding tightly onto my solar plexus. Yes, I wanted to strangle him for being cruel and cavalier to that animal that I have taken such good care of."

Staying in touch with the facts of the incident, the patient finds a metaphor for his physical experience that communicates clearly to both therapist and patient the physical correlates involved and at the same time conveys his responsibility for strangling himself as he wanted to strangle his son.

Developing linguistic refinement and precision may take simpler forms. The therapist may request that a patient experiment with finding more direct expressions of anger than barbed questions. A patient who says, "I don't understand how you could be so insensitive to me. Why did you forget my birthday?" may be encouraged to make contact with and express his anger. Saying, "I am hurt and mad that you didn't think of my birthday" is to the point of his reaction. Questioning his wife regarding the reasons for her oversight is not. It veils his feelings in seemingly intellectual inquiry. When we are confused about what we feel, we do not aid ourselves by resorting to this kind of indirection. We will not likely be satisfied, no matter what reasons are given. What he wants is not reasons, but concern.

One point of this is to help the patient find a style of expression that is sufficiently laden with affect, nuance, and metaphor to be a useful tool in explicating his experience. This becomes especially important in our attempts to know another. Our words can become a major vehicle for this kind of contact, bridging the gap of the privacy of our experience, and bridging it back again, as we find words to tell the other we understand. He knows I have heard him when he can recognize his world in my words.

Another aim of this kind of work is to refine our expression so that we can contact or recontact past experiences. They can also bring us to ourselves. The Gestalt techniques of relating past events in the present tense as we speak of them have this in mind. Speaking as though it is happening now, we reactivate the experience, making it possible for us to grasp it totally by making it a present-tense occurrence. For success, this kind of activity requires that we articulate our experience.

"My boyfriend stood me up Wednesday. It isn't a big thing, but I was very angry, I guess. I'm not, now — people are like that."

Contacted in the present tense, her generalized depression becomes present unfinished business. "Bill," she says to her boyfriend, in fantasy, "you weren't there and I am really annoyed at you. You don't put yourself out for me, as though you take me for granted and don't really care about me."

In this experience are the seeds for new growth, the possibility that this patient can confront her lover with her feelings, signifying they are important to her, and take the risk of finding out whether Bill is interested in her. By recontacting this incident, she gains the choice of acting out her sense of her own worthlessness by depressing herself, or dealing with her boyfriend.

Language can be part of the process of increasing our awareness of ourselves. Even talking about why we have acted as we have may enrich our experience. Sometimes Gestalt therapists will encourage talking about the procedures used in Gestalt therapy — techniques like changing "It is sad" to "I am sad," or retelling a past event in the present. Discussing the reasoning behind these procedures acknowledges the importance of intellection as part of the total organismic process, and gives a patient support for taking risks.

This use of words as a kind of digestive process is also an attempt to provide some insurance that the characteristic procedures of Gestalt therapy will be integrated into the patient, and not become merely newly introjected material that the patient puts on like a new set of clothes. That kind of change is not growth, but merely substituting a dependency on the style of Gestalt therapy for older dependencies. Gestalt techniques are so commanding that this is a real danger, and serious and thorough discussion can ease the possibility that the therapy will degenerate into a new escape from self on the part of the patient by imitating the therapist.

But the caution remains, that we must not confuse intellectual understanding gained through words for curative therapeutic change. This is an organismic process that changes us *in toto*, so that we are a different person. Words alone are usually not enough to effect personal growth.

(An exception to this is found in advanced stages of therapy, when self-awareness and patient-therapist contact are profound and clear enough so that speech is at one with feelings and the physical. At those times, a few apt phrases, or thoughtful, prolonged discussion may themselves evoke organismic change.)

The Role of the Therapist

> As in all cases of functional disorders, the personal relationship between doctor and patient is of prime importance. "Every sickness is a musical problem," said Novalis, "and every cure a musical solution."
>
> — *W. H. Auden*

In the previous chapter we saw that the development of abnormal functioning proceeds in stages. First we interfere with our spontaneous behavior, producing the impasse. Out of the impasse comes phobic behavior designed to avoid the ingredients that might again precipitate that seemingly unresolvable conflict, and also a veneer of social behavior intended to allow us to do the best we can, given the limitations we have imposed on ourselves.

In therapy, the process is reversed. We begin by contacting the superficial layers of avoidance and the inauthentic. Gradually we make contact with the polarities of our impasses. When we have discovered the aspects of the impasse, it dissolves into new behavior, the resurgence of our free functioning addressed to the issue at hand.

The dissolution of the impasse was called (by F. S. Perls) the exposition, or the explosive layer. It is more accurately the release of the tension we have built up by our self-conquest pouring into the figure. We may explode into anger, but we may also explode into creative action, or orgasm, or (as in the example of the woman who dreamed of her dead mother, quoted earlier) into grief.

This last stage releases us — it gets us underway again. It is explosive by contrast with our prior felt experience of impasse, like orgasm after the building up of sexual energy, or drinking after a longstanding thirst. But this explosion is different that a burst of long repressed rage. That is acting out, as we have defined it earlier, the fury of a pressure cooker with no safety valve that finally splits a seam. The explosion that is the resolution of sound therapeutic work is different. It reforms the field — it does not destroy it.

The tools that Gestalt therapists use in this process are awareness, experiment, and encounter. These aspects of the methodology of Gestalt therapy are used according to the particular requirements of each therapeutic moment. Sometimes the therapist functions as a technician, pointing the patient to new awareness and new risks. Sometimes the meeting between the therapist and patient is the primary focus of the therapeutic work, so that the therapist's skills focus on the encounter.

It is necessary for the Gestalt therapist, like any therapist, to be in touch with himself, in touch with the patient, in touch with the requirements of the moment. Good therapy requires that the therapist practice what he preaches. He must be in good contact with the field. The therapist must be centered in his own self-process and also aware of the events at his contact boundary, the encounter with the patient. This encounter goes on even when it is not the prime focus of attention.

Furthermore, the therapist must contact with the patient in the present moment and at the same time incorporate into it the theoretical framework outlined in these pages. Mostly, he must keep in touch with the gestalt dialectic — the interaction of polarities. That is his perspective. It is not something he can retreat to. It must be an assimilated, integral part of how he contacts the world, an aspect of his self.

The central and ruling attitude that guides the Gestalt therapist in applying the methodology of Gestalt therapy is that what is necessary is to find a way for the patient to take the next step in his awareness. Anything goes, if it contributes to the subtle increment of awareness that is the next step the patient is — eager, and tremulous — ready to take. "Magic in therapy is a question of timing" (L. Perls, 1972). Physical contact, authenticity, yes; but selective authenticity, appropriate to the demands of the moment, and physical contact that is unforced and apt.

Q: Are all the feelings, history, and problems of the therapist, if shared with the patient, of therapeutic value?
A: "In Gestalt therapy, we share verbally with the patient only what will promote awareness, at the next increment. Too much creates projection, flight, desensitization, resistance, anxiety" (L. Perls, 1970, p. 127).

As we have pointed out earlier, a standard repertoire of Gestalt techniques will not suffice here for the graduated and individually tailored work to be done. Techniques emerge out of the needs of each situation. The therapist must be as unique as each moment. If he copies another therapist, or continually falls back on gambits that have worked well in the past, he becomes mechanical, in-authentic, irresponsible. Of course, this is not to say that the therapist never does the same thing twice — and yet, in a way, he never does the same thing twice. If he is attuned to the present, his role is fresh, even as it is a repetition of an earlier activity. In touch with the present moment, the past cannot repeat itself.

P: I am very unhappy at home. My husband doesn't love me, I have no friends, I am always tired.

T: You know, when I listen to you complaining like that, I get tired. I feel like I want to go to sleep, or do something else, or pick a fight with you.

P: I don't like you saying that. It is unkind.

T: I'm unkind. You complain so I will be kind to you.

P: Yes.

T: It doesn't work.

P: I see.

Here the therapist shares her awareness of her own experience, accentuating the patient's contact with what is outside her, insisting she pay attention to what she communicates and how another responds to her. While stimulating the patient's awareness, the therapist also meets the patient, one person to another. In this case, therapist as awareness-technician and therapist as authentic-human-being-in-encounter are one.

Diagnosis

In sickness men have types; in health, all are unique.
— *Perls, Hefferline, and Goodman*

We saw in the example cited above a characteristic of this woman's behavior, part of her style of abnormal functioning; she attempts to make others help her by making them feel sorry for her; instead, she makes herself miserable and drives others away.

We have said earlier that Gestalt therapy eschews the formal psychiatric diagnostic labels and the mentality that goes along with it. But we can see here that a kind of typology has a place in Gestalt methodology. The typology is of process, not person. In Gestalt therapy, behavior is characterized. Patterns are underlined. To the extent that they are regular and repeated, the therapist points out the repetition. If this woman continued to manipulate others as she did in the example above, the therapist would continue to underline the parameters of her behavior, making her aware of how she frustrates herself repeatedly. When the behavior ceases, or responsibility is taken for it, the typing will stop, having served its purpose.

Diagnosis in Gestalt therapy is underlining the patterns of the patient's behavior and of his interactions with the therapist. In the course of the therapy, as the patient changes, the characterizations change. He is not stuck forever with a label, for the label does not refer to some unchanging part of his psyche, as traditional psychodiagnostic labels do, but to current behavior and attitudes.

Therapists, all therapists, find that certain patients are more deeply committed to their pathology than others. Traditionally, we say that people who are very committed to their impairment are characterologically impaired. In addition to the dimensions of contact and predominance of id or ego self-functioning, which we have said distinguishes the various abnormalities, impaired functioning is more deeply ingrained in some people than in others.

This is taken into account in the diagnostic process. The therapist continually evaluates the extent of the incremental step the patient is able to take in the development of his awareness, and at what point experimentation ought to begin. The emphasis is on what the patient can do, what he cannot do, and how large are the steps in between. In the course of the therapy, the way a patient deals with experiments and with the therapist will indicate the relative importance to him of his pathological functioning vis-a-vis more centered, contactful, and spontaneous behavior. These indications will guide the therapist's actions. Therapy proceeds more slowly when the patient's personality is predominantly balanced toward his impairment.

"Transference," and the Present Moment

The Gestalt therapist attempts to provide a situation where the patient's typical techniques of adjustment become subject to scrutiny. So, in the example cited earlier, the female patient's complaints did not elicit the sympathy she wanted. In many other therapies, the kind of interaction that was evidenced by the fragment of a therapy transcript reproduced is called transference. Simply, transference behavior is when the patient treats the therapist (or any other person) as though they were someone else. Usually it is behavior developed with a parent of the patient, and used now with anyone with whom it is successful. In psychoanalysis, and other therapies that take their cue from it, such material is significant for the light it sheds on the relationship between the patient and his parents, for understanding the nature of those relationships is the point of the therapy. In Gestalt therapy, these issues are considered issues of present contact and lack of contact. If the patient deals with the therapist as though he is the patient's parent, he is not in the present, with the therapist, and his behavior indicates a block in his awareness — he cannot distinguish between the fantasy of his father and the reality of the therapist.

P: I am afraid to say this, but I think the paint on your office door is very ugly.

The therapist asks the patient to amplify his statement.

P: That green is gross, like a hospital wall. It doesn't fit the house.

And the patient's fear?

P: I am afraid you will be angry at me.

T: What will I do?

P: You will yell at me, or not help me, or tell me I am stupid, or ask me to leave and not return.

T: And then what will happen?

The therapist elicits the full extent of the patient's present feelings.

P: I will feel lost, and abandoned. And angry, too. I am angry now, at your tossing me out for such a little thing.

The therapist suggests an experiment

T: Look at me, and tell me what you see.

P: I see your bald head, your brown eyes. They are looking at me. You are looking at me. You are smiling at me.

A pause; different expressions flit across the patients face.

T: Yes?

P: I feel silly. I guess you are not angry.

The patient laughs. The therapist laughs.

Therapist and patient may go on to discuss the interaction they have just combined, drawing out the implications of the patient's initial reaction in terms of his associations to earlier life experiences and his current behavior with others. If they talk further about it, it will be to cement this new awareness of the difference between contact with the actual and the patient's expectations. The point of the work is to increase awareness and contact.

The encounter between patient and therapist is frequently the focus of the therapeutic work. As in this example, their interaction provides opportunities for increasing the awareness of the patient. Here, the patient has come to know, once again, that the therapist is not his fantasy of his father. The transference is examined continuously in Gestalt therapy. In Gestalt terms, the here-and-now contact between the therapist and patient is one of the basic means of increasing the awareness of the patient. Through this actual encounter, the patient learns the difference between the insistent beckoning of the past and the freedom and clarity of the present.

Helping

One of the complexities inherent in any therapeutic situation concerns the nature of the help a therapist gives a patient. On the one hand, a patient comes to a therapist for assistance because there are significant aspects of his life that afford him no satisfaction, or outright pain. On the other hand, we have seen that impairment is characterized by an infantility that is seen in the patient's manipulation of his environment to reduce his involvement in the gestalt process. He is always getting help — that is his problem.

Many therapists make this seeming paradox explicit. The patient is in therapy because he needs help from the therapist, but in the therapeutic work, the patient is told that he will have to do it himself; only he can cure himself.

We have remarked earlier in this chapter that success in Gestalt therapy requires the therapist to be skilled in providing the kind of frustrations that will induce the patient to find his own resources and solutions. This is one application of the general Gestalt approach to the issue being raised here.

Another application is in the guidelines set out earlier concerning the importance of organizing the therapeutic work so that the patient's attempts to increase his awareness occur in modulated increments. The general approach to this issue in Gestalt therapy springs from the Gestalt conception of what health is. Health is self-support, reliance on the dialectic of gestalt formation and destruction. The patient must have the kind of help that eventuates in his giving up the therapist's help in favor of his own self-process. That is the only kind of permissible help. "The very worst thing you can do for people is to help them" (Glasgow, 1971, p. 65). Helping is not helpful.

As a consequence, the Gestalt approach avoids a reliance on techniques of therapy — interpretation is one example — that fosters this kind of dependency. From the Gestalt point of view, giving the patient the answers to his problems circumvents the development of the patient's own skills. Incrementally, the patient finds his own answers; until then, he has only the ones he came to therapy with. Giving the patient answers is the therapist acting as kind parent, feeding the patient as baby, so baby won't suffer and won't be unhappy, won't struggle, won't work. In this kind of exchange, the therapist remains the wise and beneficent parent and the patient remains a patient — mouth open, helpless, needing to be fed. "Solutions in therapy or elsewhere which are not born of conflict but are given by the therapist have little energy or figure" (Perls, Hefferline, and Goodman, 1951, p. 358). They cannot meet the patient's real needs, his needs for growth and the realization of his potential.

Actually, another aspect of the Gestalt understanding of behavior also makes this kind of assistance undesirable. The point of the therapy is not to make solutions, it is to make the problem-laden present more actual, by increasing the patient's awareness. The therapy cannot be focused directly to solutions, but only to increasing the possibilities for figure formation. Solutions come when we are fully in the present moment, for then our free functioning is activated. Working on our awareness invites solutions, but that is all we can do. The rest comes, of itself.

(Awareness cannot be given either, but the Gestalt therapist must guard against urging aspects of awareness on the unwilling or unprepared patient: "Look, why aren't you in touch with your anger? I am angry just sitting here listening to you." This is the Gestalt version of being dangerously helpful — feeding the patient awareness.

While it is true that refraining from feeding the patient interpretations, solutions, or awareness also avoids the risk of misleading the patient, of foisting on the patient needs and solutions that do not suit him, that is really beside the point. If the therapy were always to give the right answers, the therapist would still be misleading the patient by fostering the latter's infantility.)

Modalities of Gestalt Therapy

Gestalt therapy has been adapted to a variety of settings — to schoolrooms and art and modern dance studios, to organizations and institutions, and to natural and intentional communities. As a psychotherapy, it is used in individual, group, couple, and family therapy, in workshops, and in crisis intervention and community mental health settings.

The mode of Gestalt therapy that is in most common use, especially on the West Coast, is the workshop format developed by Fritz Perls. Basically, this arrangement permits the therapist to work with one patient at a time, surrounded by observers. Perls worked in this way with groups of from ten to several hundred. He made many films and tape recordings of his work, and nearly all of them were done in a workshop setting.

Perls himself felt that the workshop format obviated the need for individual and group therapy by combining the best aspects of both. For him, given his particular style of work and his intentions, the workshop format had many advantages. Workshops are relatively inexpensive for participants. They allow a large number of people to participate in experiments that, it is hoped, will give all of them some measure of awareness they did not have before. If the workshop consists solely of individual work in a group setting, the observers can participate indirectly, gaining some measure of insight and understanding from what they see, and the participants may do therapy in a situation whose public nature may add to the intensity of the therapeutic work. And, of course, the format allowed Perls to expose great numbers of people to Gestalt therapy.

But Perls overstated the case for workshop therapy. It limits group interaction, neglecting the importance of relationship, social systems, and contact with the world outside the individual in favor of work with the individual's dreams, fantasies, and present experience of himself. Further, individual work in a group is not the same as individual work without a group. The group situation is a dramatic one, with a built in audience which is part of anything that happens in that setting. It is hard to avoid the pressure to put on a good show and please the crowd, and sometimes this is not in accord with the next step in the patient's growth. Therapeutic work is sometimes interesting only to the therapist and patient, and the conflict between the needs of the work and the interest level of the spectators can be a cause of difficulty in the workshop format.

In the workshop, the group is mostly passive and receiving, like TV watchers; the therapist, on the other hand, is quite active. This arrangement can defeat certain of the objectives of Gestalt therapy: helping people to lead their own lives and make themselves and their environment over to suit their needs and the present possibilities. The format is structured to minimize active learning and growth.

Workshops are usually time limited arrangements. Groups usually meet for a few hours, a few days, a few weeks, maybe a few months. A further limit of this arrangement as it has been used is its implicit message that a few good experiences can replace the steady hard work of sustained personal growth. As Perls said, getting turned on by a powerful experience is not a substitute for the discipline and perseverance which are necessary for us to make profound alterations in our lives. The process of change takes time.

The more traditional therapy group, where the interaction of the members in conjunction with the therapist is the major force for personal growth, is almost nonexistent in West Coast Gestalt therapy, but it flourishes elsewhere — in New York, Cleveland, and Atlanta.

There are regional styles of Gestalt therapy. West Coast Gestalt was developed single-handedly by Fritz Perls, and Gestalt therapists there tend to work as he did in his last years. In Cleveland and New York, where Gestalt activity dates from the late forties and early fifties, Gestaltists tend toward a more interactive Gestalt group therapy, long term therapy, a greater respect for intellection, and a greater variety of personal styles of doing Gestalt therapy.

West Coast Gestalt therapy tends to pay more attention to issues of individual responsibility, centering, and self awareness. In this, it reflects Perls' emphasis on the necessity of differentiating the elements of the field as a prerequisite for good gestalt formation. In order for us to be related meaningfully to the people and things which constitute our environment, we must be defined and developed ourself. In contrast, eastern Gestalt therapy tends to put greater weight on the importance of the rest of the field and the individual's contact with it, without neglecting the other important aspects of figure formation and destruction. In this, it reflects the interactional, social and community interests of Laura Perls, Elliott Shapiro, Paul Goodman and the rest of the original New York members, and the Cleveland group.

We cannot spend much time describing the ways in which the methodology of Gestalt therapy is applied to groups, couples, families, organizations, and the like. We should note that the principles laid out in this chapter and earlier in this monograph continue to guide the Gestalt therapist working in these different settings. Awareness, contact, support, encounter, experimentation, and the concept of incremental change are the basic tools.

What is different about group work is the scale of the interaction and the nature of the ties that bind the members of groups. Polarities in group interactions tend to be divided up among the group members, rather than existing under one skin. But the dynamic of polar interaction and resolution is the same. When more people than one are involved in the therapy, the nature of their relationship to each other becomes as important as the relationship of the therapist and patient in individual therapy. Again, the dynamics of interaction are similar, though more complex.

The scale of interaction also changes in group work, especially in work with larger groups, communities, and institutions. Responsibility is diffuse, contact is harder to make, the perspective is no longer one to one, I and thou. Now it is I and them, and it is more difficult to encompass a group with the same befriending that is signified in the I-Thou relationship. Working with the staff of a community mental health center or a center for drug abusers is not the same as individual psychotherapy. There are great differences in scale, motivation, and expectations. But the Gestalt approach is a mentality, a considered way of understanding how we function in the various contexts in which we find ourselves. The methodology comes out of the approach, and the techniques come out of the methodology.

The Gestalt therapist comes to new situations with an attitude developed out of his training and experience, and a confidence that the process of gestalt formation and destruction that is the common process of human beings can produce satisfactory solutions to the dilemmas and challenges of our lives. Gestaltists

bring this mentality to their own living and to the various professional and personal situations in which they find themselves.
They are not always being therapists, but they contact the world in
terms of the attitudes that have been set forth in these pages — in
terms of the lively fluidity of contact and interaction, gestalt
formation and destruction, and awareness.

Chapter 6
THE LAST GESTALT

Religions, political and philosophical systems, and schools of psychological theory usually come into being out of a vision that stems from a unique personal, and intellectual viewpoint. There is a certain passion that informs the development of the ideas and experiences of a man or a group of men, keeping them focused from the time of their origination through their final expression. It is our contact with the quality and depth of our visions that is our constant reference point in the process of creation.

However, we often find that these new gestalts — political concepts, spiritual values, psychological approaches — usually suffer in the hands of their adherents. The multiplication of interest in any school of thought or interest seems inevitably to attract those who lack the motivation or ability to grasp its essential aspects. We know familiar instances of this phenomenon: the advocates of Christian living whose stern prohibitions disallow the exercise of love; the Marxists who view the working class with respect and workers with uneasiness; the physician who takes the Hippocratic oath and fails to see the humanity of the person who comes to him, needing his help.

Granted, this is a difficult task: to pass on faithfully the basis of a way of understanding and being so that it stimulates a similar vision within another person. It is difficult for the teacher, and difficult for the student. It seems that our imperfections and the difficulties of the task often conspire to make its outcome an unsuccessful one.

Problems in the Practice of Gestalt Therapy

Gestalt therapy has not been immune from this process of losing contact with the living origins of its attitude. Some of what is called Gestalt therapy bears only a superficial resemblance to the work of its more astute, faithful, and inspired practitioners.

A familiar problem in Gestalt therapeutic work is one we touched on before: confusing the simple physical expression of what has been repressed with the final goal of therapy — spontaneous free functioning. Take the example of an upper-middle-class suburban housewife who feels she has slowly been dying in her routine of taking care of her husband and taking care of her children. In the course of therapy, she becomes aware of a great deal of resentment toward her family, her parents — who taught her how to be a good wife and mother — her women friends, who seem oblivious of their bondage and support hers, and to men. "I'm just fed up with doing things for other people and never having time for myself. I'm indispensable, all right, like a toilet is."

In our terms, she is discovering elements of the field that she had not known before. As new feelings, these resentments have a primacy because of their immediacy and power. They shoulder out older feelings that are also a part of her — her love for her family, for example. It is likely that she will be expressing some of those new feelings not only in therapy but outside of it as well, evidencing her anger directly to her friends and family. This is probably inevitable, and from our point of view it is also desirable. She is making her feelings part of the world she lives in, and unifying her feelings and their expression.

But we should also remember, given our understanding of the gestalt process, that she is developing the other side of the polarity. Her former behavior — her felt submission to the wishes of others, her excessive femininity, her helplessness that dominated her behavior — is being opposed by her new and growing sense of having left herself out of the picture, resenting it, and wanting to express this new aspect of herself. That is, this new behavior is the necessary next step on her way to a workable resolution of this polarity. It is not health, it is not integrated behavior.

A problem occurs here if the therapist does not recognize that these new feelings represent the remainder of the field, complementing the patient's earlier feelings. If these new feelings are taken to be the "real" feelings of the patient that have previously been repressed, or if they are taken to be the resolution of the dialectic, a disservice is done to the process and to the patient. The aspects of Gestalt therapy emphasizing organismic spontaneity and experimentation are taken out of the context of the ongoing gestalt process of creating figures out of the organism/environment field and making creative adjustments within that field. The resulting outbursts of resentment only dissipate energy. They don't make for the next new gestalt in her life. They leave her out of touch with the world she lives in and the particular circumstances out of which her resentment developed. The patient is encouraged to trade one pole of her internal conflict for the other, and the working through process of gestalt formation and destruction is aborted.

This particular dynamic of insufficiently thorough Gestalt work is a common one. But we can see that the difficulty is not in the methodology of the therapy but with faulty execution. Patient and therapist have mistaken a milestone on their journey for the destination. Two societal factors seem to contribute to this kind of error. First, we live in, and are perhaps emerging from, a cultural situation where behavior characteristically is quite inhibited. Especially in the middle classes, the style of impairment that predominates is based on the repression of many impulses and their replacement by reason and deliberation. Hence, the emergence of strong and clear feelings is an attractive and desirable event. Being able to produce and experience intensely feelings of hate and love, sadness and dissatisfaction is a breath of fresh air in the closed room of rationalization and confusion. Indeed, many people — patients and therapists — are drawn to Gestalt therapy because it is willing to acknowledge the importance of sensation and emotions in our lives. In this context, it is easy to see how we get stuck here, on the other side of the fence.

Another factor, closely related to the first, is also clearly illustrated by this example. The conflict seems to be between the patient's sense of her own needs and desires and her sense of the needs and desires of others. The poles are contact with the self and contact with the environment, the inner zone versus the outer. Again, our social context usually places a greater weight on the side of the expectations that others have of us. This begins for most of us in childhood. And it is liberating for us to discover that we have feelings of our own and that we can make our own desires and interests count. But we should remember that this represents only the seesaw of these two poles. It is acting out the inner zone polarity, not the resolution of both sides into unified functioning.

Another place where Gestalt therapists seem to go astray from sound practice is closely related to the ones we have been looking at. We have stressed the importance of being responsible for our actions and experience. We are, each of us, responsible for what we do. Our acts, our thoughts, our feelings are all part of us. Our experience defines our existence. WE are this person who is feeling, thinking, being right now.

This emphasis on our own part in the living of our lives is a salutary counterbalance to the social and personal alienation in and around us. But Gestalt therapists sometimes take it a little too far. Instead of functioning in middle mode, in the flow of our lives, we see statements like "No one, nothing influences me without my consent."

Fritz Perls warned against the attitude implicit in this statement (and in some of the problematic work we referred to above). It bespeaks an attitude that he called a "false humanism," wherein each of us is an isolated willful being who controls everything that exists in our world. It is grandiose and inaccurate, a protection and reaction against the vagaries of contact with things outside us. It is, again, a playing out of one side of a polarity — in this case, the polarities of free will and determinism, or our control over our life and others' control of it, or (as it sometimes turns out) child and parent. Its synthesis is the paradox that we are at the same time the center of our universe and also participants in its ceaseless pulsation. Taking our lives in our own hands, we come to see how intimately we are related to all the other aspects of the world we live in. Both independence and interdependence are aspects of our place in the field.

Perls spoke against another abuse of Gestalt therapy in his last years.

> We are entering the phase of the turner-onners: turn on to instant cure, instant joy, instant sensory-awareness. We are entering the phase of the quacks and the con-men, who think if you get some break-through, you are cured — disregarding any growth requirements, disregarding any of the real potential, the inborn genius in all of you. If this is becoming a faddism, it is as dangerous to psychology as the year-decade-century-long lying on the couch. At least the damage we suffered under psychoanalysis does little to the patient except for making him deader and deader. This is not as obnoxious as this quick-quick-quick thing. The psychoanalysts at least bring good will with them. I must say I am *very* concerned with what's going on right now.

This is also in many respects a cultural phenomenon, the consequence of the ingenuity of our technology. We live in a push-button age. In four hours we can fly from New York to San Francisco. On a psychedelic trip we get enlightenment. Turn on the television and we are in touch with the other end of the world. Take a pill and we become relaxed, or energized, or blissful. Common to these experiences and attitudes is their speed and the passivity of our involvement with them. We are instantly transformed or transported, with little or no effort on our part. As we have seen, sound growth and serious therapy do not work in that fashion — rather they require discipline, persistence, and often the ability to tolerate pain. But in our milieu, there are many attempts made in the guise of therapy — Gestalt and otherwise — that subscribe to these new cultural values.

One way this is evidenced by some who call themselves Gestalt therapists is in a rigid adherence to a few dramatic techniques. Bypassing the training and understanding that are the foundation of a thorough grasp of Gestalt therapy, they mistake the appearance of the therapy — its powerful and accessible techniques — for its substance. Instant Gestalt therapy. "One of the objections I have against anyone calling himself a Gestalt therapist is that he uses technique. A technique is a gimmick," says Perls. This shallow therapy "...often becomes a dangerous substitute activity, another phony therapy that *prevents* growth.''

It is important to underline these instances of faulty work in Gestalt therapy in order to distinguish between Gestalt therapy and therapy that has a superficial resemblance to it. We have been speaking not of limitations or problems in the Gestalt approach, but of mistaken and misguided attempts to understand and use it. We might conclude by looking at a different sort of problem in Gestalt therapy. Actually, it is not so much a problem as a consequence of a particular attribute of the Gestalt approach. We noted earlier that the perspective of Gestalt therapy is directed primarily on the processes and structures of organismic behavior. If, for example, we examine a telephone conversation, we will pay particular attention to the quality of communication involved: the particular qualities of the voices we hear, the absence of visual information, elements of clarity, directness, and syntax in the speech of the two parties. We will be less interested in the subject of the conversation. Our conversationalists may be talking about horse racing, but our concern is largely with the way they do this rather than with horse racing itself. In this way, Gestalt therapy can be seen as a palliative to approaches that are predominantly concerned with the subject matter of behavior — the psychoanalytic emphasis on sexuality, for example, or analytical psychology's focus on the common mythic elements of modern man's activities and attitudes.* We are especially interested in the way figures are created and destroyed, and less interested in the particulars of the figures.

This attitude can make a significant contribution to all the disciplines that study man. It spotlights the processes that animate the forms taken by aspects of our culture, or by other cultures. But at the same time, if it is used so that paying attention to content is excluded, we make a problem for ourselves. We overlook the pertinence of history and culture. Processes never occur outside a context. People talking on the telephone are not just talking; they are talking about horse racing, or children, or politics, or music.

---

*In fact, Jung's work contains the same basic outline of our processes that we have described here. But for him and his followers, processes are background, and content is foreground. In Gestalt therapy, the reverse is true.

The Last Gestalt

Growth consists of being able to form gestalts of greater and greater complexity. As infants, we start out with the figures formed of our primeval needs. The components of the field are few and our facility in manipulating them minimal. As we grow, we begin to be able to integrate other elements into our functioning. Our senses become more refined. We become able to walk, to run, and to speak. We gain in strength and mobility. The quality of our contact with the field becomes more varied, forceful, and subtle.

We can see the same dynamic of growth and development operate in therapy. In therapy we expand our awareness to include new aspects of the field. Enlarging our possibilities, we concomitantly create solutions that are more encompassing and more complex. Therapy is a process of embracing together more and more of our own potential and the potential of the rest of the field.

Making gestalts is making wholes. It is the process of unifying disparate elements. As we grow, we become capable of organizing more and more of the field into wholes. Functioning freely, we do not stand apart from this process. The wholes we make include ourself. We are part of the unity of the field.

The farther reaches of this process are traditionally matters for philosophy and religion. The prospect of our coming to experience ourself as intimately related to our fellow men, to nature, to life, to the cosmos, even to our most catastrophic creations, and the ways by which that unification can be achieved have been the fundamental interests of religious leaders, philosophers, and theologians. Psychology has also taken an interest in our spiritual aspirations and development since its inception as a modern discipline. In spite of a general commitment to a peculiarly impersonal brand of scientific inquiry on the part of the field, some psychologists — Jung and his followers, especially, in the early years of this century, many others later — have defined psychology and psychotherapy so that it recognizes the importance of our continued growth beyond the categories of mental health and mental illness, neurosis and normality, sickness and well-being.

In our terms, this direction is toward the last gestalt. The momentum of our development is toward wholes that encompass more and more of the potential of the organism/

environment field. In the more advanced stages of this process, we are embracing ourself and the cosmos. The gestalt is: I and the universe are one. All of me and all of the infinity of activities and energy around me, people and things, all of them together are one figure. Nothing is excluded.

Sitting here, this volume is related to me, I to my chair, my chair to the floor, the floor to the house, and on and on to all the human beings, all the objects in the world — and to the sky, the stars, and the rest of everything. The last gestalt is beginning to know the immensity of the extent of our interaction with everything else. As we read, we move our eyes — and the whole interconnected universe moves. The last gestalt is apprehending this viscerally, body, mind, and soul, to the depths of our being, leaving nothing out.

READINGS
IN GESTALT THERAPY

This section contains a bibliography of Gestalt therapy, a complete roster of published writings, tapes, and films, and a sampling of important but harder to obtain materials.

The following selections, taken from the bibliography, are especially recommended to the reader interested in going on from the present volume.

GESTALT THERAPY. *Perls, Hefferline, and Goodman.*

This collaboration is perhaps the single most important book in Gestalt therapy. The first half contains applications of Gestalt principles in the form of therapeutic exercises. The second half is a stimulating, difficult, and provocative exposition of the theory of Gestalt therapy. It is slow going; some readers are put off by its denseness, and others find it enriching.

GESTALT THERAPY NOW. *Fagan and Shepherd, Eds.*

This collection gives a good indication of the range of people and styles working in Gestalt therapy. Especially recommended are the contributions by Fritz Perls, Wallen, Polster, Enright, Laura Perls, Fagan, and Shepherd.

GESTALT THERAPY VERBATIM. *Frederick S. Perls.*

Verbatim was done in the last few years of Perls' life. Consisting of transcripts of lectures and therapy sessions he gave, it is mostly a demonstration of his idiosyncratic and compelling style of Gestalt therapy. It often reads like a pop novel, one exciting event following another. This is the place to go if you want to be turned on to Gestalt therapy.

EGO, HUNGER, AND AGGRESSION. *Frederick S. Perls.*

This was written nearly thirty years before *Verbatim*. Where the latter attracts because of the dramas being played out on its pages, *Ego, Hunger, and Aggression* is exciting for its wealth of insight into psychotherapy and the processes of health and sickness, and for the breadth of its intellectual interests.

GESTALT THERAPY INTEGRATED. *Erving and Miriam Polster.*

A book about doing Gestalt therapy. Using examples and discussion, the authors relate theory and practice with a view toward helping practitioners understand and use Gestalt therapy.

A Bibliography
of Gestalt Therapy

Beisser, A. (1970). Paradoxical theory. In J. Fagan and I. Shepherd (Eds.), *Gestalt therapy now* (pp. 77-80). Palo Alto: Science and Behavior Books.

Bloomberg, L. and Miller, R. (1968). Breaking through the process impasse. *Voices, 4*(3), 33-36.

Brown, G. I. (1969). Awareness training and creativity based on Gestalt therapy. *Journal of Contemporary Psychotherapy, 2*(1), 25-32.

Clements, C. (1969). Acting out versus acting through: An interview with Frederick Perls. *Voices, 4*(4), 66-73.

Close, H. (1970). Gross exaggeration with a schizophrenic patient. In J. Fagan and I. Shepherd (Eds.), *Gestalt therapy now* (pp. 154-156). Palo Alto: Science and Behavior Books.

Cohn, R. (1970). A child with a stomachache: Fusion of Psychoanalytic concepts and Gestalt techniques. In J. Fagan and I. Shepherd (Eds.), *Gestalt therapy now* (pp. 197-203). Palo Alto: Science and Behavior Books.

Cohn, R. (1970). Therapy in groups: Psychoanalytic, Experiential and Gestalt. In J. Fagan and I. Shepherd (Eds.), *Gestalt therapy now* (pp. 130-139). Palo Alto: Science and Behavior Books.

Creelman, M., Fredericson, E., Polster, E., Ritz, G., Wallen, R. (1958). *Gestalt therapy, theory and applications.* Presentation at the Convention of The Psychological Association of Ohio.

Denner, B. (1970). Deception, decision-making and Gestalt therapy. In J. Fagan and I. Shepherd (Eds.), *Gestalt therapy now* (pp. 301-308). Palo Alto: Science and Behavior Books.

Ennis, K., and Mitchell, S. (1970). Staff training for a day care center. In J. Fagan and I. Shepherd (Eds.), *Gestalt therapy now* (pp. 295-300). Palo Alto: Science and Behavior Books.

Enright, J. (1970). Awareness training in the mental health professions. In J. Fagan and I. Shepherd (Eds.), *Gestalt therapy now* (pp. 263-273). Palo Alto: Science and Behavior Books.

Enright, J. (1970). An introduction to Gestalt techniques. In J. Fagan and I. Shepherd (Eds.), *Gestalt therapy now* (pp. 107-124). Palo Alto: Science and Behavior Books.

Enright, J. (1971). *Thou art that: Projection and play in Gestalt therapy.* San Francisco: Lodestar Press.

Fagan, J. (1970). Anne: Gestalt techniques with a woman with expressive difficulties. In J. Fagan and I. Shepherd (Eds.), *Gestalt therapy now* (pp. 169-193). Palo Alto: Science and Behavior Books.

Fagen, J. (1970). The tasks of the therapist. In J. Fagan and I. Shepherd (Eds.), *Gestalt therapy now* (pp. 88-106). Palo Alto: Science and Behavior Books.

Fagen, J. and Shepherd, I. (1970). *Gestalt therapy now*. Palo Alto: Science and Behavior Books.

Fantz, R. n.d. *Fragments of Gestalt theory*. Cleveland: Gestalt Institute of Cleveland.

Glasgow, R. (1971, November). Paul Goodman, a conversation. *Psychology Today,*, 62-96.

Goldstein, K. (1963). *The organism, a holistic approach to biology derived from pathological data in man*. Boston: Beacon Press.

Goodman, P. (1960). *Growing up absurd*. New York: Random House.

Goodman, P. (1965). Essay. In S. Gorovitz (Ed.), *Freedom and order in the university*. Cleveland: Case Western Reserve University.

Goodman, P. (1966). *Five years*. New York: Random House.

Goodman, P. (1968a). The golden age. In P. Pursglove (Ed.), *Recognitions in Gestalt therapy* (pp. 129-145). New York: Funk and Wagnalls.

Goodman, P. (1968b). Human nature and the anthropology of neurosis. In P. Pursglove (Ed.), *Recognitions in Gestalt therapy* (pp. 64-83). New York: Funk and Wagnalls.

Greenwald, J. (1969). An introduction to the philosophy and techniques of Gestalt therapy. *Bulletin of Structural Integration, 1*(3), 9-12.

Greenwald, J.(1969). Structural integration and Gestalt therapy. *Bulletin of Structural Integration, 1*(4), 19-20.

Kempler, W. (1967). The experiential therapeutic encounter. *Psychotherapy: Theory, Research and Practice, 4*, 166-172.

Kempler, W. (1970). Experiential psychotherapy with families. In J. Fagan and I. Shepherd (Eds.), *Gestalt therapy now* (pp. 150-161). Palo Alto: Science and Behavior Books.

159

Kepner, E. (1965, May). (Review of Cassette Recording #18), E. Sagen (Speaker), Gestalt expressive therapy. *American Academy of Psychotherapists Newsletter, 10*(2).

Kepner, E., and Brien, L. (1970). Gestalt therapy: A behavioristic phenomenology. In J. Fagan and I. Shepherd (Eds.), *Gestalt therapy now* (pp. 39-46). Palo Alto: Science and Behavior Books.

Knight, W. A. (1967). Gestalt therapy and pastoral counseling. *Pastoral Counselor, 5*(1), 16-21.

Kogan, J. (1972). *Gestalt therapy resources*. San Francisco: Lodestar Press.

Latner, J., and Sabini, M. (1972). Working in the dream factory. *Voices, 8*(3), 38-43.

Lederman, J. (1969). *Anger and the rocking chair: Gestalt awareness with children*. New York: McGraw-Hill.

Lederman, J. Anger and the rocking chair. In J. Fagan and I. Shepherd (Eds.), *Gestalt therapy now* (pp. 285-294). Palo Alto: Science and Behavior Books.

Levitsky, A. and Perls, F. S. (1970). The rules and games of Gestalt therapy. In J. Fagan and I. Shepherd (Eds.), *Gestalt therapy now* (pp. 140-149). Palo Alto: Science and Behavior Books.

Marcus, H. (1970). The probation officer and Gestalt therapy techniques. *Journal of the California Probation, Parole and Correctional Association, 7*(3).

Naranjo, C. (1968). I and thou, contributions of Gestalt therapy. In H. A. Otto and J. Mann, (Eds.), *Ways of growth*. New York: Grossman.

Naranjo, C. (1969). *The unfolding of man*. Palo Alto: Stanford Research Institute.

Naranjo, C. (1970). Present-centeredness: Techniques, prescription and ideal. In J. Fagan and I. Shepherd (Eds.), *Gestalt therapy now* (pp. 47-69). Palo Alto: Science and Behavior Books.

Naranjo, C. (1980). *Techniques of Gestalt Therapy*. Highland, NY: The Gestalt Journal.

Nevis, E. n.d. *Beyond mental health*. Cleveland: Gestalt Institute of Cleveland.

O'Connell, V. (1967). Until the world becomes a human event. *Voices, 3*(2), 75-80.

O'Connell, V. (1970). Growth psychotherapy: Person, dialogue, and the organismic event. In J. Fagan and I. Shepherd (Eds.), *Gestalt therapy now* (pp. 243-256). Palo Alto: Science and Behavior Books.

Pearson, L. (1970). *A demonstration of Gestalt therapy*. Atlanta: Human Development Institute.

Perls, F. (1969). *Ego, hunger, and aggression*. New York: Random House. (First published in 1947, London: Allen and Unwin).

Perls, F. (1948). Theory and technique of personality integration. *American Journal of Psychotherapy, 2*, 564-586.

Perls, F. (1951). (Introduction). In J. Winter, *A doctor's report on dianetics, theory and therapy*. New York: Julian Press.

Perls, F. (1953). Morality, ego boundary and aggression. *Complex, 9*, 42-51.

Perls, F. (1975). Workshop vs. individual therapy. In J. Stevens, (Ed.), *gestalt is*, (pp. 9-16). Moab, UT: Real People Press.

Perls, F. (1970a). Dream seminars. In J. Fagan and I. Shepherd (Eds.), *Gestalt therapy now* (pp. 204-233). Palo Alto: Science and Behavior Books.

Perls, F. (1970*b*). Four lectures. In J. Fagan and I. Shepherd (Eds.), *Gestalt therapy now* (pp. 14-38). Palo Alto: Science and Behavior Books.

Perls, F. n.d. *a*. *Dream sessions*. Big Sur: Esalen Recordings

Perls, F. n.d. *b*. *Dream theory and demonstration*. Big Sur: Esalen Recordings.

Perls, F. (1978). Finding the self through Gestalt therapy. *The Gestalt Journal, 1*(1), 54-73. (First presented at Cooper Union Forum Series on "The Self," New York City).

Perls, F. n.d. *d*. *Frederick Perls' Gestalt therapy*. Orange, CA: Psychological Films.

Perls, F. n.d. *e*. *Fritz Perls reads portions of his unpublished autobiography*. Big Sur: Esalen Recordings.

Perls, F. n.d. *f*. *Fritz's circus*. Big Sur: Esalen Recordings.

Perls, F. n.d. *g*(Speaker). Gestalt therapy. In E. Shostrom, *Three approaches to psychotherapy* (Film). Orange, CA: Psychological Films.

Perls, F. n.d. *h*. *Gestalt therapy and human potentialities*. Cleveland: Gestalt Institute of Cleveland.

Perls, F. n.d. *i*. *Gestalt therapy lectures*. Big Sur: Esalen Recordings.

Perls, F. n.d. *j*. *Gestalt therapy seminar*. Salt Lake City, UT: AAP Tape Library.

Perls, F. n.d. *k*. *More dream sessions*. Big Sur: Esalen Recordings.

Perls, F. n.d. *l*. *A session with college students*. Orange, CA: Psychological Films.

Perls, F., Hefferline, R., and Goodman, P. (1965). *Gestalt therapy*. New York: Dell. (First published by Julian Press, New York, 1951).

Perls, F., Hefferline, R., and Goodman, P. (1969). Gestalt psychotherapy. In W. Sahakina, *Psychotherapy and counseling.* New York: Rand McNally.

Perls, F. (1968a). *The birth of a composer.* San Diego: Media-Psych.

Perls, F. (1968b). *The case of Mary Kay.* San Diego: Media-Psych.

Perls, F. (1968c). *The death of Martha.* San Diego: Media-Psych.

Perls, F. (1968d). *Demon.* San Diego: Media-Psych.

Perls, F. (1968e). *Grief and pseudo-grief.* San Diego: Media-Psych.

Perls, F. (1968f). *The impasse.* San Diego: Media-Psych.

Perls, F. (1968g). *Relentless greed and obesity.* San Diego: Media-Psych.

Perls, F. (1968h). *A session with college students.* San Diego: Media-Psych.

Perls, F. (1968i). *The treatment of stuttering.* San Diego: Media-Psych.

Perls, F. (1971). *Gestalt therapy verbatim.* New York: Bantam Books. (First published, Moab, UT: Real People Press, 1969a).

Perls, F. (1969b). *In and out the garbage pail.* Moab, UT: Real People Press.

Perls, L. (1950, summer). The psychoanalyst and the critic. *Complex, 2,* 41-47.

Perls, L. (1968). Notes on the psychology of give and take. In P. Pursglove (Ed.), *Recognitions in Gestalt therapy* (pp. 118-128). New York: Funk and Wagnalls.

Perls, L. (1968). Two instances of Gestalt therapy. In P. Pursglove (Ed.), *Recognitions in Gestalt therapy* (pp. 42-63). New York: Funk and Wagnalls.

Perls, L. (1962). The Gestalt approach. *Annals of Psychotherapy, 1 and 2.*

Perls, L. (1970). One Gestalt therapist's approach. In J. Fagan and I. Shepherd (Eds.), *Gestalt therapy now* (pp. 125-129). Palo Alto: Science and Behavior Books.

Perls, L. n.d. *Some aspects of Gestalt therapy.* New York: Unpublished manuscript.

Polster, E. (1957, May). Paper presented at seminar on Gestalt therapy, Mid-West Psychological Association, Chicago.

Polster, E. (1970). A contemporary psychotherapy. In P. Pursglove (Ed.), *Recognitions in Gestalt therapy* (pp. 3-19). New York: Funk and Wagnalls.

Polster, E. (1967). *Techniques and experience in Gestalt therapy.* Paper presented at The Convention of the Ohio Psychological Association. (Also Cleveland: Gestalt Institute of Cleveland).

Polster, E. (1967, February). *Trends in Gestalt therapy.* Paper presented at the Ohio Psychiatric Association, Cincinnati. (also Cleveland: Gestalt Institute of Cleveland).

Polster, E. (1967, September). *The integrative effect of social psychotherapy*, proceedings of 75th Annual Convention, American Psychological Association, Washington, D.C.

Polster, E. (1970). Sensory functioning in psychotherapy. In J. Fagan and I. Shepherd (Eds.), *Gestalt therapy now* (pp. 70-76). Palo Alto: Science and Behavior Books.

Polster, E. (1971). Encounter in community. In A. Burton (Ed.), *Encounter.* San Francisco: Jossey Bass.

Polster, E. n.d. *Instructor's outline—methodology of Gestalt therapy.* Cleveland: Gestalt Institute of Cleveland.

Polster, E., and M. Polster. (1973). *Gestalt therapy integrated.* New York: Brunner/Mazel.

Pursglove, P. (Ed.). (1968). *Recognitions in Gestalt therapy.* New York: Funk and Wagnalls.

Reich, W. (1960). *Selected writings, an introduction to orgonomy.* New York: Farrar, Strauss, and Giroux.

Rhyne, J. (1970). The Gestalt art experience. In J. Fagan and I. Shepherd (Eds.), *Gestalt therapy now* (pp. 274-284). Palo Alto: Science and Behavior Books.

Rhyne, J., and Vich, M. (1969). Psychological growth and the use of art materials: Small group experiments with adults. In A. Sutich and M. Vich (Eds.), *Readings in Humanistic psychology.* New York: Free Press. (First published in *Journal of Humanistic Psychology, 7,* 163-170, 1967.)

Rosanes, M. (1970). Gestalt therapy as an adjunct to treatment for some visual problems. In J. Fagan and I. Shepherd (Eds.), *Gestalt therapy now* (pp. 257-262). Palo Alto: Science and Behavior Books.

Rosenberg, J. (1971, July). A Gestalt approach to thumb sucking. *Arizona State Dental Journal.*

Rosenberg, J. A. (1971, June). Gestalt awareness for apprehensive patients. *Dental Survey,* 48-55.

Rosenberg, J.A. (1971, December). The human potential trip: Awareness training for professionals. *California Dental Journal.*

Sagan, E. (1965, November). Creative behavior. *Explorations, 4,* 8-15.

Sagen, E. n.d. (Speaker). *Gestalt expressive therapy.* (Tape recording). Salt Lake City, UT: AAP Tape Library.

Schlicter, J. (1968). Movement therapy. In P. Pursglove (Ed.), *Recognitions in Gestalt therapy* (pp. 112-117). New York: Funk and Wagnalls.

Shepherd, I. (1970). Limitations and cautions in the Gestalt approach. In J. Fagan and I. Shepherd (Eds.), *Gestalt therapy now* (pp. 234-238). Palo Alto: Science and Behavior Books.

Shostrom, E. (1968). *Man the manipulator*. New York: Bantam Books. (First published in Nashville: Abington Press, 1967).

Simkin, J.(Ed.). (1968). *Festschrift for Fritz Perls*. Los Angeles.

Simkin, J. (1970). Mary: 2 sessions with a passive patient. In J. Fagan and I. Shepherd (Eds.), *Gestalt therapy now* (pp. 162-168). Palo Alto: Science and Behavior Books.

Simkin, J. n.d. (Speaker). *a. Individual Gestalt therapy..* (Tape recording). Salt Lake City, UT: AAP Tape Library.

Simkin, J. n.d. (Interviewer). *b. Interview with Dr. Frederick Perls*. Salt Lake City, UT: AAP Tape Library.

Simkin, J. n.d. (Speaker). *c. In the now*. (Film). Orange, CA: Psychological Films.

Simkin, J. n.d. *d. An introduction to the theory of Gestalt therapy*. Cleveland: Gestalt Institute of Cleveland.

Stevens, B. (1969). *Don't push the river*. Moab, UT: Real People Press.

Stevens, J. (1971). *Awareness*. Moab, UT: Real People Press.

Tobin, S. A. (1969-1970, winter-spring)). Self support, wholeness, and Gestalt therapy. *Voices, 5*(4),5-12.

Van Dusen, W. (1968). Existential analytic psychotherapy. In P. Pursglove (Ed.), *Recognitions in Gestalt therapy* (pp. 29-41). New York: Funk and Wagnalls. (First published in *American Journal of Psychoanalysis, 20*, 1960, 35-40.)

Van Dusen, W. (1967). The theory and practice of existential analysis. *American Journal of Psychotherapy, 11*, 310-322. (First published in H. M. Ruitenbeek (Ed.), *Psychoanalysis and existential philosophy*. New York: Dutton, 1962.)

Walker, J. L. (1971). *Body and soul: Gestalt therapy and religious experience*. Nashville: Abington Press.

Wallen, R. (1970). Gestalt therapy and Gestalt psychology. In J. Fagan and I. Shepherd (Eds.), *Gestalt therapy now* (pp. 8-13). Palo Alto: Science and Behavior Books. (Original manuscript, Cleveland: Gestalt Institute of Cleveland, n.d.).

Zinker, J. (1966). Notes on the phenomenology of the loving encounter. *Explorations,10*, 3-7.

Zinker, J. (1968, October). On public knowledge and personal revelation. *Explorations, 15*, 35-39. (Original manuscript, Gestalt Institute of Cleveland, paper No. 10, n.d.)

INDEX

THE AUTHOR

Joel Latner, Ph.D., is a clinical psychologist in private practice in Rochester, New York, who has been involved in Gestalt therapy for nineteen years. After a tenure on the teaching faculty of the Gestalt Institute of San Francisco and several years as Clinical Director of the Graduate Program in Clinical Psychology and Assistant Professor of Psychology at Lone Mountain College in San Francisco, he became the founding director of the Central California Gestalt Therapy Training Program. More recently, he founded and directs the Gestalt Therapy Institute of Rochester. He has also taught Gestalt therapy at several other training centers and universities. Dr. Latner has published a number of articles on aspects of Gestalt therapy, and has presented and participated at a variety of professional conferences. He is a member of the editorial board of *The Gestalt Journal*, the professional publication in Gestalt therapy. At the present time, he lives with his wife, Laurie, and three of his four children in Rochester, New York.